Homeless and Policed:

The Racialized Policing of Urban Homeless Mobility

JOSHUA FREISTADT, PHD

Publisher:
Joshua Freistadt
P.O. Box 1051
Pilot Butte, Saskatchewan, Canada
S0G 3Z0
joshua.freistadt@outlook.com

ISBN: 978-0-9958082-0-1

DEDICATION

"We may be homeless, but we are not heartless"
-Staci, White homeless female

"They don't see the person that is fucking suffering. … I think people should be compassionate with each other."
-Carl, Aboriginal homeless male

This research is dedicated to all the street-involved individuals who shared their stories with me. It is my sincere hope that their stories might change hearts, produce sympathy, multiply compassion, and inspire new responses to homelessness.

CONTENTS

ACKNOWLEDGMENTS

My sincere thanks to the street-involved individuals who agreed to speak with me about their personal lives. I am also indebted to the colleagues, reviewers, and research committee members who provided insightful comments on earlier versions of this book. Of course, any errors or omissions are my own. Finally, but above all, my deepest appreciation goes to my wife, Lindsay, and our two children, Hailey and Thomas. Their encouragement and patience was invaluable throughout this long project.

This research would not have been possible without the financial support of the Social Science and Humanities Research Council of Canada, the Killam Trusts, the City of Edmonton, and the Department of Sociology at the University of Alberta. The views expressed herein are those of the author alone.

The research reported here has also supported the following publications:

Hogeveen, Bryan & Joshua Freistadt. (2013). Hospitality and the homeless: Jacques Derrida in the Neoliberal City. *Journal of Theoretical and Philosophical Criminology*. 5(1): 39-63.

Freistadt, Joshua. (2016). No Dumping: Indigenousness and the racialized police transport of the urban homelessness. In Evelyn Peters and Julia Christensen (Eds.), *Indigenous Homelessness: Perspectives from Canada, Australia, and New Zealand*. Winnipeg: University of Manitoba Press.

INTRODUCTION

ELI'S CRY: HEAR THE HOMELESS AND POLICED

Eli is an Aboriginal panhandler and bottle picker in his mid-50s who lives in Edmonton, Alberta, Canada.[1] We met midway through my field research in the summer of 2011. He was asking for money outside a liquor store on the east end of Whyte Avenue, just beyond the popular retail and entertainment strip that caters primarily to White consumers and young university students. He sauntered toward me with his head downcast and his faded hat hiding his bruised face. When asked, "How's it going?" Eli got right to the point. "Not too good," he sadly replied. "I really need a drink. Can you spare change?"

We spent the morning talking while sitting on inverted five-gallon buckets in the dilapidated parking lot behind his daughter's apartment building. Eli taught me about his past, hopes, and everyday life on the streets. He gives the meager income assistance he gets to his daughter and granddaughter so they can rent the small suite inside. Meanwhile, he stays on the street and survives off the money he makes picking bottles and panhandling. His face was bruised because other street-involved persons assaulted and robbed him for the $70 he made panhandling the previous day.

Colonialism, racism, and trauma drove Eli to despair and alcoholism. As a boy, Eli lost his entire immediate family in a fiery tragedy. He has suffered episodic depression ever since. Orphaned, government workers removed him from his Reserve and placed him in the foster care of a White family.

---

[1] All research participants have been assigned pseudonyms.

With teary eyes Eli recalled, "When I was in the foster home, my foster mom was mean to me. She called me a nigger and everything. She told me, 'You are a fucking Indian. … You are an asshole. You belong out there.'" Although he loved the rest of his foster family dearly, the abuse he received from his foster mother pushed him out onto the streets.

Eli has lived on the streets since he was a young teenager. He said that security guards chase him away from commercial establishments. Several of these businesses proudly hang posters dissuading customers from giving money to panhandlers. He explained that police officers occasionally fine and jail panhandlers but thus far have chosen to repeatedly escort him off Whyte Avenue and take him to his daughter's apartment building, the city's shelters, or other social services. Despite the fact that few people welcome him on the streets of Old Strathcona, Eli considers the area home. He fears most other neighbourhoods. As we parted company Eli chillingly told me, "This is where I stay. I will not get off the street. I will die here on the street."

Eli rejected my offer to take him to an agency that helps the homeless and said he would prefer to continue panhandling. He bemoaned that although he has visited countless agencies over the years only one social worker ever took the time to hear his story. He was happy to have discussed his life with a second person, despite the difficult emotions evoked during our interview. When asked what he wanted for the future, Eli did not say money, alcohol, stable housing, addictions treatment, or better social services. Rather, he thoughtfully stated, "I want respect." He desired recognition above all else.

Topic: The Experiences of Heavily-Policed Homeless Persons

This book takes Eli's cry for recognition and respect seriously. It uses interviews with Eli and 21 other homeless adults to improve understandings of the contemporary policing of homelessness. Participants' stories question the enforcement of anti-panhandling bylaws, the use of informal police move-outs and move-alongs, and the proliferation of campaigns that try to usher the homeless into crises-oriented social services. I argue that the stories of the homeless reveal that Edmonton's new anti-panhandling efforts make problematic assumptions about street life and contribute to a racialized policing of homelessness, space, and mobility. Although Edmonton, Alberta, Canada provides the context for this research and contains a unique spatial and racial organization, several of the arguments provided here could easily extend to the many other cities that have formally outlawed activities related to homelessness, informally policed homeless mobility patterns, and created campaigns to dissuade charitable donations to panhandlers.

This research contributes to scholarship about the policing of homelessness by integrating the stories of participants into the major debates. My analyses support arguments that contend the policing of homelessness helps constitute consumer spaces (e.g., Feldman, 2004, Mitchell, 1997, 2004) but I argue that scholars must also recognize how this policing is racialized (e.g., Comack, 2012) and produces everyday mobility patterns that protect the interests of businesses, police agents, and White individuals. I thus use the voices of the homeless to integrate literatures on the experience of homelessness (e.g., Wardhaugh, 1996), the racialization of space (e.g., Razack, 2002a, 2002b), and the politics of mobility (e.g., Cresswell, 2006, 2010, 2012) into arguments about the policing of homelessness (e.g., Wilson & Kelling, 1982; Gordon, 2006, 2010; Mitchell, 1997, 2004; Blomley, 2012). As I will show throughout this book, the stories of the homeless raise important questions overlooked by most studies of the policing of homelessness.

This introductory chapter sets the stage for these arguments and demonstrates the importance of critically investigating the policing of homelessness and experiences thereof. I argue that different approaches to homelessness are desperately needed and that hearing the voices of homeless persons can help develop improved responses. First, I define homelessness and briefly review its extent and causes. Second, I conceptualize policing and discuss how a growing number of cities have opted to respond to increased visible homelessness through bylaws and diverted giving campaigns. Third, I detail how these measures developed in Edmonton and so provide the backdrop for this study. I conclude by documenting the dire conditions of homelessness and arguing that attending to these conditions involves acknowledging the lived experiences of the homeless under conditions of heavy policing. In so doing I provide the general research question that animates this book.

The Extent and Causes of Homelessness

I define homelessness as living "without stable shelter on an absolute or temporary basis" (O'Grady, Gaetz & Buccieri, 2011, p. 37). This definition includes persons who are absolutely homeless (i.e., without any form of shelter) and individuals who are relatively homeless (i.e., housed precariously in emergency shelters, relatives' houses, or substandard housing) (Minaker & Hogeveen, 2009). For this study I spoke with members of both groups who spent their daytime hours in outdoor public spaces. This included people without any source of stable shelter, individuals with temporary beds in emergency shelters, and "street-involved" persons who were tenuously housed yet remained involved in the informal economy and still associated with street-based networks (MacLaurin & Worthington, 2012, pp. 280-281).

Enumerating homeless people is difficult for a variety of reasons: those without property evade typical survey methods, there are multiple definitions of homelessness, homelessness is often a temporary or episodic occurrence, and some homeless people remain out of public view (Echenberg & Jensen, 2008). Nevertheless, research consistently reports that since the 1970s the number of people like Eli has drastically increased across Canada (Hulchanski, Campsie, Chau, Hwang & Paradis, 2009; O'Grady, Gaetz & Buccieri, 2011; Lenon, 2000), the United States (Beckett & Herbert, 2009; Rahimian, Wolch & Koegel, 1992), and the United Kingdom (Jordan, 1999). Although precise statistics are difficult to pin down, the construction of homelessness as a social problem testifies to the increased numbers of unsheltered persons within developed nations. When Eli first turned to the streets roughly 40 years ago, the number of people without access to adequate shelter was so low that policy makers did not yet have a term to conceptualize the issue (Hulchanski, Campsie, Chau, Hwang & Paradis, 2009). Today, in contrast, Eli shares his condition with somewhere between 200,000 and 300,000 absolutely or relatively homeless Canadians (Laird, 2007) and "homelessness" is a well-recognized, albeit diverse, phrase policy makers use to refer to this social problem (Hulchanski, Campsie, Chau, Hwang & Paradis, 2009).[2]

Eli's story highlights the well-researched causes and pathways of homelessness. Although the backgrounds of homeless people are diverse, alcoholism and drug abuse, familial disruption, abusive homes, psychological issues, and child welfare involvement often precede homelessness (Gaetz & O'Grady, 2002; Kidd, 2012; Minaker & Hogeveen, 2009; Tanner, 2009). The increased number of homeless Canadians since Eli first hit the streets also demonstrates how social and economic policy changes over the past four decades contribute to homelessness. More people in developed nations have lost housing since the 1970s due to economic restructuring that has dismantled the social safety net, stagnated wages, eliminated cost sharing for housing and health between different levels of government, diminished direct government investment in affordable housing, outsourced low-skill jobs to countries with cheaper labour, and deinstitutionalized mental health treatments (Beckett & Herbert, 2009; Hulchanski, Campsie, Chau, Hwang & Paradis, 2009;

---

[2] "While it is true that all societies through history tend to have some people who are homeless – without a home – we have not always had the set of social problems we associated with the word homelessness" (Hulchanski, Campsie, Chau, Hwang & Paradis, 2009, p. 6).

Jordan, 1999; Lenon, 2000; Lyon-Callo, 2000; O'Grady, Gaetz & Buccieri, 2011; Rahimian, Wolch & Koegel, 1992).

Aboriginal persons such as Eli are among Canada's most marginalized and so are particularly vulnerable to the negative effects of this socio-economic restructuring. In Canada Aboriginal people are vastly overrepresented among the absolute and relatively homeless (Belanger, Weasel Head & Awosoga, 2012; Hulchanski, Campsie, Chau, Hwang & Paradis, 2009; Lenon, 2000). Jurisdictional limbo, inadequate housing on Reserves, insufficient housing and social supports for Aboriginal peoples in urban centres, over-incarceration, and high rates of family disruption and violence stemming from assimilationist polices like the Residential School system contribute to this overrepresentation (Belanger, Weasel Head & Awosoga, 2012; Hulchanski, Campsie, Chau, Hwang & Paradis, 2009; Peters, 2012; Peters & Robillard, 2009). Indeed, it is well documented that a "full-blown national Reserve-housing crisis" has existed since the mid-1960s due to inadequate federal funding for housing initiatives on Reserves (Belanger, Weasel Head & Awosoga, 2012). Poor housing conditions on Reserves draw some Aboriginal persons into urban centres (Peters, 2012; Peters & Robillard, 2009) where they often cannot secure adequate housing because of market prices and discrimination from landlords (Hulchanski, Campsie, Chau, Hwang & Paradis, 2009). Moreover, both on and off Reserves colonial efforts to remove traditional ways of life have jeopardized the domestic relationships of many Aboriginal households, leaving inter-generational histories of substance abuse and family violence that understandably push some Aboriginal persons to the streets (Minaker & Hogeveen, 2009).

The lingering effects colonialism has on homelessness are readily apparent in Edmonton where only five percent of the total population identifies as Aboriginal, yet Aboriginal people comprise forty-six percent of the visibly homeless population (Sorensen, 2012). Thus, while "there is no one face of homelessness" (Hulchanski, Campsie, Chau, Hwang & Paradis, 2009, p. 10), Eli, as an Aboriginal male, represents a familiar figure.

Policing Responses to Increased Homelessness

The causes and pathways into homelessness that Eli's story illuminates demonstrate that homelessness is not a criminal justice issue but instead a product of social policy failure, reliance on market-based housing, social welfare restructuring, colonialism, and personal trauma. Nonetheless, many cities, often inspired by the broken windows theory of policing (Wilson & Kelling, 1982; Kelling & Coles, 1997), have deployed legal responses to address the growing numbers of visibly homeless persons (Beckett & Herbert, 2009; Feldman, 2004; Mitchell, 2004; O'Grady, Gaetz & Buccieri,

2011). Provincial, state, and municipals laws and bylaws criminalize different behaviours associated with homelessness – like loitering, drinking, urinating, or sleeping – when they are done in public (Duneier, 2001; Hermer, 1997; Mitchell, 2004; O'Grady, Gaetz & Buccieri, 2011). Don Mitchell (1997) aptly refers to these different laws as anti-homeless ordinances since they outlaw things we all do – sleep, defecate, seek money – but are only enforced in public spaces such that they aim predominately, if not exclusively, at the homeless population.

In many North American cities such anti-homeless ordinances target the informal economic activities homeless persons complete to make ends meet (Berti & Sommers, 2010; Blomley, 2011; Collins & Blomley, 2003; Ferrell, 2006; Hermer & Mosher, 2002; Mitchell, 2004). These informal economic activities consist of income-generating actions such as panhandling (begging), squeegeeing (windshield cleaning), street vending, and recycling. All of which occur in public space, exist outside paid employment, are not taxed, and are not covered under criminal law but are often policed as signs of urban disorder (Gaetz & O'Grady, 2002). Often laws dealing with this informal economy restrict the ways and places in which persons can ask for material aid (Blomley, 2011; Collins & Blomley, 2003; Hermer & Mosher, 2002; Mitchell, 2004). For instance, Ontario's Safe Streets Act (1999) and British Columbia's Safe Streets Act (2004) make it illegal for persons to panhandle for money in aggressive fashions or within proximity of bank machines, pay phones, stopped cars, and bus stops (Hermer & Mosher, 2002; Berti & Sommers, 2010; O'Grady, Gaetz, & Buccieri, 2011). Winnipeg, Saskatoon, Halifax, Calgary, Montreal, and several other major Canadian cities have created municipal bylaws with similar anti-panhandling provisions (Collins & Blomley, 2003).

The development of anti-panhandling laws and other anti-homeless ordinances is more than a symbolic gesture that admonishes the impoverished. Loic Wacquant (2012, 2009) attributes a significant proportion of the United States prison expansion to the widespread use of policing strategies that aim at the urban disorders anti-homeless laws condemn. William O'Grady, Stephen Gaetz, and Kristy Buccieri (2011) demonstrate that the Toronto Police have excitedly deployed Ontario's Safe Streets Act (1999). Despite a decrease in the numbers of visibly homeless on Toronto's streets, the number of tickets Toronto police officers have issued under Ontario's Safe Streets Act (1999) has increased 2,147 percent, "from 710 tickets in 2000 ... to 15,224 in 2010" (O'Grady, Gaetz & Buccieri, 2011, p. 10). Similarly, from 1994 to 2010 Montreal police officers increased the number of bylaw infractions they issued to homeless persons six-fold. In 2010 homeless persons were charged with three-quarters of all bylaw infractions issued on the island of Montreal ("Montreal police", 2012). Because 98 percent of bylaw tickets to the homeless go unpaid, the tickets translate into astronomical processing costs for the criminal justice system and jail time or burdensome debt for the homeless (O'Grady, Gaetz & Buccieri, 2011).

In many cities police officers have employed other tactics to manage the visibly homeless. Demands that homeless persons "move-along" have been long-standing informal ways to respond to complaints about homeless persons (Dean & Melrose, 1999; Golub, Johnson, Taylor, & Eterno, 2003, p. 690; Hermer, 1997; O'Grady, Gaetz & Buccieri, 2011). In some cities, police officers have physically escorted homeless persons out of areas and dropped them off in remote locations where they are unlikely to generate complaints (Feldman, 2004; King & Dunn, 2004). In other cities, police officers have argued that the encampments of homeless persons constitute litter and have collected and destroyed the belongings of the homeless (Feldman, 2004).

While anti-homeless ordinances and direct police action have been the favoured responses, burgeoning homeless populations have also inspired other approaches less obviously connected to law enforcement. Several cities have developed public education campaigns that attempt to eliminate panhandling by convincing the public they should not give money to the homeless but instead ought to direct the homeless and donations to social services. For instance, after judges decided that escorting persons who looked homeless out of New York City's Penn Station was illegal, security officials developed posters telling individuals not to give money to the homeless (Duneier, 2001). In Winchester, England, instead of telling passersby not to give money, business owners developed a "diverted giving campaign." They erected charity boxes alongside sidewalks with messages that compelled passersby to give to agencies that help the poor instead of giving directly to panhandlers (Hermer, 1999). The Downtown Business Association in Calgary has utilized similar campaigns (Mayers, 2001). One of its recent public education posters showed a person injecting drugs and read, "Your generosity is killing me. Give spare change to agencies instead of panhandlers" (Klaszus, 2010).

Policing involves all the above responses. Although the most common image of police is that of the uniformed force working to detect and prevent crimes, policing has always entailed discretion in the application of laws (such as anti-homeless ordinances) and the use of informal police responses (such as move-alongs) (Griffiths & Hatch Cunningham, 2003). Moreover, the history of policing – as both a science and practice – depicts a much broader scope than the actions of officers alone (Donzelot, 1979; Dubber & Valverde, 2006; Foucault, 1991; Neocleous, 2000). "Police" and "policy" share common etymological roots (Neocleous, 2000) such that policing is best understood as the more general internal administration of a state's population (Donzelot, 1979; Foucault, 1991; Neocleous, 2000).

Indeed, members of some early police forces completed many regulatory functions beyond the detection of crimes. British officers around the 15th century not only dealt with crime but inspected health conditions, enforced minimum wages, acted as domestic missionaries searching for vice within households, and provided food and shelter to the "deserving" poor (Donzelot, 1979; Gordon, 2006; Neocleous, 2000). Today people associate many of these tasks with social policy and social work because states have compartmentalized specialized police functions (Donzelot, 1979; Neocleous, 2000). "[I]n light of their historical, conceptual, and political concordance," however, considerations of police, social policy, and social work "should in fact be studied together" (Neocleous, 2000, p. 724).

This book therefore broadly conceptualizes the policing of homelessness as attempts to administer and regulate the street-involved population on the part of formal police agents, social workers, and social policy makers. Formal police agents means those employed to protect the public. This includes sworn peace officers, transit officers, and private security. Discussions about social work predominately concern charitable agencies that operate at an arm's length from government bodies. Finally, while there is a range of social policies used to address homelessness, the focus of this research is on diverted giving campaigns and, to a somewhat lesser extent, policies related to urban planning and redevelopment. Diverted giving campaigns form the book's primary engagement with social policy because as educational social policies supported by social workers, formal police agents, government officials, and business leaders, these campaigns exemplify "the broad powers and remit of police" alongside the "complex network of institutions" and interests through which policing operates (Neocleous, 2006, p. 18).

Edmonton's Policing Responses

Eli's story conveys the policing efforts adopted by many cities struggling with large visibly homeless populations. In 2010 Edmonton City Administration brought into force a revised Public Places Bylaw (2009) which subjects aggressive panhandlers to $250 fines. The City of Edmonton, however, was aware that anti-poverty activists were developing court challenges for some the spatial restrictions found in other anti-panhandlings laws and so developed a bylaw that did not prohibit panhandling in specific spaces but instead targeted behaviours that allegedly make panhandling aggressive (Kent, 2009, p. A1). The bylaw reads:

> 4.1 (1) A person shall not panhandle in an aggressive manner in any public place.
>
> [...]
>
> (3) For the purpose of this section, and without limiting the generality of the phrase, a person shall be considered to be   panhandling in an "aggressive manner" if they:
>> (a) obstruct or impede the passage of another person;
>> (b) make continued requests or solicitations after receiving a negative response from another person;
>> (c) insult, threaten, coerce or intimidate another person;
>> (d) make physical contact with another person; or
>> (e) are intoxicated by alcohol or under the influence of illegal drugs;
>
> while panhandling.[3]

The bylaw thus defines aggressive panhandling by referring to several unruly actions that might accompany requests for aid. These acts include obstructing, harassing, intimidating, and physically contacting passersby. If those seeking aid do so while intoxicated, this definition of aggressive panhandling also applies regardless of outward behaviour. While Eli had not yet received a fine under the new bylaw, several of his friends had not escaped ticketing.

Business and police representatives typically instigate drives to develop the anti-homeless ordinances Eli must navigate as he tries to survive on the streets (Beckett & Herbert, 2009; Berti & Sommers, 2010; Duneier, 2001; Mitchell, 2004). In Edmonton, business leaders had advocated for an anti-panhandling bylaw since at least the early 1990s. The most vocal anti-panhandling proponents were the Downtown Business Association and the Old Strathcona Business Association. These agencies represent the business interests of the two regions where Edmonton's visibly homeless are most apparent (see Kent, 1992, p. B2; Retson, 1998, p. B7). It was only in 2008, however, that the Edmonton Police Service (EPS) began to push City Administration for an explicit anti-panhandling bylaw. Prior to the revised Public Places Bylaw (2009), EPS officers relied on the obstruction provisions of the Traffic Bylaw (2007) and informal responses that ushered panhandlers out of commercial centres or asked the homeless to move-along (Pallas, 2008). Starting in 2008, however, the EPS began to feel these responses were "too limiting" because they did not allow officers to "come right out and say no panhandling" (Pallas, 2008, p. 3). As such, they began

---

[3] The full bylaw is publicly available at:
http://webdocs.edmonton.ca/Bylaws/C14614.doc

to join business leaders from Downtown and Old Strathcona in lobbying for new municipal legislation.

Anti-poverty advocates and researchers publicly criticized the development of an anti-panhandling bylaw (Ferguson, 2007, p. B1; Raworth, 2007, p. A19; Wright, 2007, p. A19), but several factors aided the law's passage and motivated the EPS to join business leaders' push for a new law. First, from 1999 to 2008 the visibly homeless population in Edmonton tripled to over 3,000 (Sorensen, 2010). Over this period a red-hot economy led by the energy sector created inflationary pressures that caused rents to double (Edmonton Social Planning Council, 2007). The affordability crisis that followed led to an infamous tent city that housed upwards of 110 people. Media coverage of this homeless encampment pressured City Administration to address its homelessness problem ("Province won't tear," 2007; Zabjek, 2007, p. B1).

Second, in May 2005 a few EPS officers took nine Aboriginal panhandlers off Whyte Avenue, drove them around in a hot van for an hour and a half, ignored their pleas to be released, and dropped them off half-clothed in a neighbourhood north of Downtown. A resident of the neighbourhood did not appreciate her back yard being used as a "dumping ground for derelicts from Whyte Avenue" and reported the issue to the media (Simons, 2007, p. B1). The event was infamously referred to as the "sweatbox" incident and much of the ensuing press coverage criticized the EPS (Sadava, 2007, p. B1; Simons, 2007, p. B1). It was only after this incident that EPS officials began to argue aggressive panhandling was out of control. Utilizing unofficial counts of concerns heard through such dubious sources as "town hall meetings, emails, letters, community league meetings and business revitalization committees" (Elanik, 2009, p. 2), police told City Councillors that aggressive panhandling complaints increased 118 percent from 2008 to 2009 (Elanik, 2009). The EPS used these claims in an attempt to persuade city councillors to approve a complete ban on "asking for money from another person" (Pallas, 2008, p. 3).

Third, the anti-panhandling bylaw had the support of some well-seasoned politicians. Edmonton's Chief of Police at the time, Mike Boyd, had substantial experience advocating for similar legislation. Prior to coming to Edmonton, Boyd worked in Toronto and was a key lobbyist behind Ontario's Safe Streets Act (1999) (McKeen, 2006, p. B1). Additionally, the popular and powerful Mayor, Stephen Mandel, introduced the panhandling issue for debate among City Council and favoured the use of a bylaw (Kent, 2007, p. A3).

Alongside the bylaw, in an effort to develop a more robust response to panhandling and to assuage the concerns of some city councillors that a new law was "overkill" that punished the poor (Linda Sloan in Ho, 2009), Edmonton's Community Services Committee decided to champion a diverted giving campaign (Anderson, 2009). City Hall established an Integrated Panhandling Unit consisting of representatives from the EPS, inner-city charitable agencies, and the business community to promote the diverted giving campaign, called "Have a Heart, Give Smart" (HHGS) (Ho, 2010). This "public education" campaign – borrowed from Seattle – utilizes posters, brochures, press releases, and a mobile outreach team to inform passersby about the dangers of giving money to panhandlers (Anderson, 2009).

Several of the businesses along Whyte Avenue where Eli panhandled proudly displayed posters from the HHGS campaign. The campaign materials tell passersby:

> Giving money to panhandlers may support drug and alcohol addictions. There are many services and supports available in Edmonton. If you really want to help people in need, please support agencies that provide food, shelter and other resources. ... Giving money to panhandlers may discourage them from accessing community resources that can help. (City of Edmonton, 2010b)[4]

The street outreach team behind this campaign visits panhandling "hotspots," hands out brochures with the above message, and provides the public with index cards that list Edmonton's homeless-serving agencies (Ibrahim, 2010, p. B3, p. B3). HHGS spokespersons and EPS officials encourage passersby to direct the homeless to the agencies on the index (Rodrigues, 2012).

The agencies to which the HHGS campaign encourages people to direct homeless persons are the same charitable organizations to which police often physically escorted Eli. In Edmonton, the bulk of these services are located in the McCauley and Boyle Street neighbourhoods (Hogeveen & Freistadt, 2013). These two abutting neighbourhoods are among the most crime-ridden in Edmonton. In 2005 McCauley and Boyle Street witnessed violent crimes rates that were almost 4 times the average rate for Edmonton (City of Edmonton, 2005a, 2005b, 2005c; Hogeveen & Freistadt, 2013). Meanwhile, the two neighbourhoods comprised the first (McCauley) and third (Boyle Street) poorest communities in the city, with median incomes that were less than half the city-wide median (Edmonton Social Planning Council, 2011). Unsurprisingly, the region also contains a disproportionately high percentage of Edmonton's subsidized housing. In fact, while 4.8 percent of the housing across Edmonton is subsidized, 61 percent of housing in the McCauley neighbourhood falls into this category (Kleiss,

---

[4] The leaflet for the HHGS campaign is publicly available at:
http://www.edmonton.ca/for_residents/Have_a_Heart_Give_Smart_leaflet.pdf

2010, p. A1). These impoverished areas have thus become the spaces in which the poor, dispossessed, and homeless like Eli are shooed.

Meanwhile, the ties between the EPS and business representatives from important consumer areas such as Old Strathcona and Downtown are evident in the development of Edmonton's anti-panhandling responses. Both the EPS and HHGS team highlight Downtown and Old Strathcona as the areas in which they will focus their policing and education efforts ("Anti-panhandling campaign," 2010; Elanik, 2009; Ibrahim, 2010, p. B3). Moreover, the HHGS campaign was first launched in Edmonton by the Old Strathcona Business Association. It was adopted by City Council after the EPS feared the anti-panhandling bylaw alone might "result in ... the perception, by some, that the city is punishing the poor and disadvantaged" (Elanik, 2009, p. 3; see also Anderson, 2009).

City Council's endorsement of an anti-panhandling bylaw and a diverted giving campaign make Edmonton an ideal setting to investigate the policing of homelessness. Eli's story points to the important role formal and informal police responses, social services, and public education campaigns play in his everyday life. Although anti-homeless ordinances abound (see, for e.g., Berti & Sommers, 2010; Collins & Blomley, 2003; Duneier, 2001; Hermer & Mosher, 2002; Mitchell, 2004), informal police responses that chase the homeless out of areas are well-recognized (see, for e.g., O'Grady, Gaetz, & Buccieri, 2011), and diverted giving campaigns are common (see, for e.g., Duneier, 2001; Hermer, 1999; Mayers, 2001), criminological scholarship typically deploys narrower definitions of policing (Neocleous, 2000) and so overlooks how these strategies simultaneously operate in the lives of the homeless population. This gap in the literature might be partly attributed to the fact that Edmonton appears to be the first municipal government to explicitly tie bylaw enforcement and diverted giving campaigns together in an integrated response to panhandling (Anderson, 2009). In other cities, diverted giving campaigns have largely remained the purview of business associations while city administrations focus predominately on anti-homeless ordinances.

Conclusion: The Dire Need to Hear Homeless Persons' Voices

The conditions of homeless populations are appalling and doing something to better attend to the needs of homeless persons is sometimes a matter of life and death. The homeless population faces shorter life expectancy and disproportionate rates of victimization, poor health, and imprisonment (Minaker & Hogeveen, 2009; O'Grady, Gaetz & Buccieri, 2011; Tanner, 2009; Thomas, 2012). Sadly, from 2007 through 2010, at least 194 homeless people died on Edmonton streets (Sands, 2008, p. A12; Drake, 2009, p. A5; Brooymans, 2010, p. A5; Liewicki, 2011, p. A7). Some of these individuals lost their lives simply because they were unable to meet their basic needs (Brooymans, 2010, p. A5). Eli's valediction that he "will die here on the streets" is thus a sad reality for many homeless persons.

In fact, despite Homeward Trust Edmonton's ability to leverage over $222 million to address affordable housing (Sorensen, 2012), the life and death dangers of homelessness continue to threaten many people. While some new Housing First funds helped shelter over 1,750 persons between 2008 and 2011 (Homeward Trust Edmonton, 2012), the official count of visibly homeless persons in Edmonton – which underestimates the amount of homelessness by as much as 80 percent (Belanger, Weasel Head, & Awosoga, 2012, p. 2) – only decreased by 905 over that same period (Sorensen, 2012). The disparity between the number of people housed and the reduction of homeless persons in the latest head count shows that considerable numbers of people continue to fall into homelessness. It also suggests that some of the individuals these programs shelter remain street-involved. While any reduction in the number of homeless persons is a praiseworthy accomplishment, clearly more needs to be done.

The persistence of homelessness among Aboriginal people like Eli is particularly disheartening. The 2012 count of homeless persons in Edmonton shows that while the numbers of homeless White persons dropped by 31 percent from its peak in 2008 (387 of 1,236), the reduction in homeless Aboriginals over that same period was only 11 percent (108 of 986) (see Sorensen, 2012). Since the proportion of Aboriginal clients in Housing First programs is roughly the same as the proportion of Aboriginal persons in the city's Homeless Count at 43 percent (see Homeward Trust Edmonton, 2012; Sorensen, 2012), this disparity in percentage reductions between Whites and Aboriginals does not indicate that homeless Aboriginal persons are being shut out of housing programs. Rather, it suggests that Aboriginal individuals have been falling into homelessness at much higher rates than other groups.

An unwillingness to listen to the voices of the homeless contributes to their persistent dire conditions. Policy is often reckless if it does not reflect the lives of those it hopes to help (Duneier, 2001). The city has not heeded the voices of people like Eli in its turn to anti-panhandling measures. In fact, when City Council developed its bylaw and HHGS campaign it scrapped initial plans to carry out a comprehensive study of panhandlers after some councillors felt listening to panhandlers would be "wasting resources" that should be used to develop solutions (Kent, 2009; see also Kent, 2010).

Ignoring the voices of homeless persons, however, narrows possible solutions. Outsiders, rather than homeless persons, frame the issue of homelessness and consequently one-size-fits all policing responses prevail. My aims in hearing the voices of the homeless are to gain a better understanding of the policing of homelessness and to imagine responses that better reflect their lived realities. While the causes of homelessness and the pathways individuals take to the streets are well-documented (Kidd, 2012; Minaker & Hogeveen, 2009; Tanner, 2009), their experiences under conditions of heavy policing are less understood (Mitchell & Heynen, 2009; O'Grady, Gaetz & Buccieri, 2011). In order to ameliorate the conditions of homelessness and make people like Eli feel welcome and respected in city spaces, researchers and policy makers must hear Eli's cry for recognition and be attune to its echoes throughout the homeless population. To this end, this book begins with the question: How do the homeless experience policing?

This question serves as a launch-point into further questions. It is, for example, a question that produces several new areas of exploration within the literature on the policing of homelessness. The next chapter further outlines my intervention in, and contribution to, the main arguments within this literature.

CHAPTER 1

CONTRIBUTION AND METHOD: ADDING THE VOICES OF THE HOMELESS TO ARGUMENTS ABOUT THE POLICING OF HOMELESSNESS

Don Mitchell and Nik Heynen (2009), alongside authors like William O'Grady, Stephen Gaetz, and Kristy Buccieri (2011, p.8), observe that arguments about the policing of homelessness seldom examine the lives of the homeless. Just as those who developed Edmonton's anti-panhandling efforts ignored the experiences and voices of the homeless, many researchers who have supported or challenged anti-homeless efforts have overlooked the stories of the street-involved. Mitchell and Heynen (2009, p. 615), for instance, note that "[t]here has been ... little synthesis between ... on-the-ground ethnographic research ... and the more abstract arguments about the relationship between antihomelessness and the right to be" (Mitchell & Heynen, 2009, p. 615). These authors thus confirm the need to investigate how homeless persons experience policing through anti-homeless efforts such as Edmonton's anti-panhandling bylaw and diverted giving campaign.

This literature review chapter makes a case for taking up Mitchell and Heynen's (2009) call to integrate more ethnographically-inspired observations into arguments about anti-homeless efforts and the place of homeless persons in public space. I argue that collecting and analyzing the stories of homeless persons can advance research on the policing of homelessness by examining how this policing unfolds on the ground, whose interests it protects, and how it is racialized. That is, listening to the voices

15

of the homeless through semi-structured in-situ interviews can contribute to the major arguments about the policing of homelessness and to the debates among these arguments about who homeless persons are, why they are policed, the politics behind this policing, and how best to respond to this policing.

This discussion unfolds in four steps. First, I outline the four dominant arguments about what the policing of homelessness does: the broken windows theory (Wilson & Kelling, 1982; Kelling & Coles, 1997), the production of the proletariat argument (Gordon, 2006, 2010), the civic sanitation argument (Berti & Sommers, 2010; Collins & Blomley, 2003; Feldman, 2004; Mitchell, 1997, 2004; Mosher, 2002), and the pedestrianism position (Blomley, 2007, 2011, 2012). This section foreshadows the contributions this book makes to these four different positions and lists some of the arguments future chapters develop. It also introduces concepts from more ethnographically-inspired research that I will inject into existing scholarly arguments, such as "marginalized" and "prime" spaces (Feldman, 2004; Wardhaugh, 1996; Wardhaugh & Jones, 1999) and the "politics of mobility" (Cresswell, 2006, 2010, 2012).

Second, I discuss how the main arguments about the policing of homelessness overlook racialization. This section draws on Sherene Razack (2002a, 2002b), Theo Goldberg (1993), and Elizabeth Comack (2012) to explain how this study understands race and racialization. It then sketches how I will document the racialized policing of homelessness.

Third, I discuss how this book taps the experiences of Edmonton's street-involved. This section outlines and defends my data collection and analysis procedures. It also describes the characteristics of participants and how I determined their racial identities.

I conclude by summarizing my intervention and discussing how the overarching argument this book develops contributes to debates within the literature on the policing of homelessness. In so doing I describe the organization of the remaining chapters.

Contributions to the Major Arguments about the Policing of Homelessness

While the research on homelessness is extensive and growing (Meanwell, 2012; Kidd, 2012), this literature review concentrates more narrowly on writing that focuses on the policing of homelessness through anti-homeless ordinances or diverted giving campaigns. Scholars have paid considerable attention to anti-homeless ordinances in general and anti-panhandling laws in particular (Beckett & Herbert, 2009; Berti & Sommers, 2010; Blomley, 2007, 2011; Collins & Blomley, 2003; Duneier, 2001; Ellickson, 1996; Gordon, 2006, 2010; Hermer & Mosher, 2002; McNeil, 2010; Parnaby,

2003; Schaefer, 1998, 2007). By comparison, diverted giving campaigns have received considerably less attention (Duneier, 2001; Feldman, 2004, p. 46; Hermer, 1999, 2001; Mayers, 2001). That few scholars have written about diverted giving campaigns reflects the fact that most researchers deploy a narrower definition of policing as the enforcement of law by uniformed officers (Neocleous, 2000).

The focus on law and formal police responses has encouraged most researchers to concentrate on the language of official documents that support anti-homeless efforts. In particular, most arguments about anti-homeless ordinances involve a critical discourse analysis of the wording of anti-homeless ordinances or the legislative and media debates that surround such laws (Blomley, 2011; Collins & Blomley, 2003; Hermer & Mosher, 2002; Mitchell, 2004; Parnaby, 2003; Schaefer, 1998, 2007). For example, Don Mitchell's (2004) extensive discussion of anti-homeless ordinances critically analyzed the language of many municipal bylaws and the newspaper reports that discussed these laws, but he did not support his arguments with any data from the homeless. Similarly, engagements with diverted giving campaigns have mainly utilized critical discourse analyses (Duneier, 2001; Feldman, 2004; Hermer, 1999, 2001; Mayers, 2001). For instance, Joe Hermer (1999), the only scholar to make diverted giving campaigns his primary focus, did not examine these campaigns from the perspective of the homeless. He critically appraised the images and language within Winchester's diverted giving program and, using interviews with the persons who developed the initiative, criticized the campaign's ability to generate funds for charities. Unfortunately, he did not talk with the homeless persons this diverted giving campaign hoped to push into charitable agencies.

The official discourses and documents (written laws, newspaper reports, campaign materials, redevelopment plans, etc.) upon which authors base their arguments often ignore or silence marginalized persons' voices (Freistadt, 2010; Hayward, 2004; Minaker & Hogeveen, 2009). Although many authors are critical of anti-homeless efforts and contend that housed citizens, politicians, and police agents ought to recognize the homeless as legitimate users of public space (e.g., Mitchell, 2004; Mosher, 2002), the homeless are themselves missing from their arguments and methodologies. As I will show throughout this chapter and this book, starting from the experiences and stories of the homeless contributes to understandings of the policing of homelessness by addressing several new questions and verifying if the conclusions scholars make based on official discourses reflect the lives of homeless persons.

Of course, several scholars have previously advocated for greater attention to how the homeless encounter law enforcement (Collins & Blomley, 2003; O'Grady, Gaetz & Buccieri, 2011; Mitchell & Heynen, 2009) and there is a growing body of research that examines the experience of homelessness (Meanwell, 2012). Some of this research has focused on the everyday routines of persons who participate in the informal economy (Gowan, 2009; Lankenau, 2009a, 2009b; Mayers, 2001), but only a handful of scholars like Mitchell Duneier (2001), Mario Berti and Jeff Sommers (2010), and William O'Grady (see O'Grady & Bright, 2002; Gaetz & O'Grady, 2002; O'Grady, Gaetz & Buccieri, 2011) discuss the policing of homelessness and collect data from homeless persons. Berti and Sommers (2010), for instance, challenge the construction of homeless persons as safety threats by using interviews with the homeless to document their high levels of victimization.

My research follows in this tradition of collecting data from the people anti-homeless efforts attempt to police. However, this book contributes to this ethnographically-inspired research by focusing more broadly on the everyday lives of the homeless and by adopting a wider conception of policing that includes the enforcement of anti-homeless ordinances by police officers, the development of diverted giving campaigns, the consequences of urban planning policies, and the informal actions of police agents. This allows for a fuller discussion of how policing, in its many manifestations, intersects with the lives of the homeless. Moreover, I use the stories of street-involved persons to appraise the major scholarly claims about the policing of homelessness. Although scholars have set forth four major arguments about anti-homeless ordinances and diverted giving campaigns, these different arguments have yet to be situated among the stories of the homeless.

The Broken Windows Theory

The broken windows theory justifies the development and enforcement of anti-homeless ordinances and so is the argument about anti-homeless efforts that has received the greatest political traction. Indeed, according to Travis Pratt, Jacinta Gau and Travis Franklin (2011), the broken windows theory is one of the most dominant ideas in municipal crime control. James Wilson and George Kelling (1982), who first articulated this position, used secondary data to conclude that signs of physical disorder, like graffiti, or social disorder, like homelessness, cause law-abiding people to fear and avoid certain areas, thereby reducing the natural surveillance of the location and inviting more criminal activity. Since minor disorder leads to fear of crime, which leads to avoidance, which allegedly causes community decline and increasing criminal activity, Wilson and Kelling (1982; see also Kelling & Coles, 1997) determined that city officials and police ought to immediately remove signs of disorder such as loitering homeless persons. Thus, according to the broken windows theory, anti-panhandling laws, diverted giving campaigns, and other policing measures that expel the homeless are appropriate crime prevention measures.

Wilson and Kelling (1982, p. 14) did not examine the lives of the homeless persons or panhandlers they argued ought to be promptly removed from areas lest a "criminal invasion" occur. Rather, they simply assumed that panhandlers and homeless persons legitimately generated fear among law-abiding citizens and so should be expelled. What are the lives of the homeless like? Should individuals fear the homeless and panhandlers? Do homeless persons encourage further crime? How are they policed?

Turning to the stories of the homeless helps attend to these questions. Chapter two highlights the parallels between broken windows theorists and the claims of those who supported Edmonton's anti-panhandling efforts. It then uses the stories of the street-involved to challenge and contextualize the image of panhandlers and homeless persons as dangerous. Additionally, throughout this book I describe and question many of the practices and arguments used to police the homeless in the name of crime prevention. Chapter three, for instance, shows that the HHGS campaign and other efforts to displace homeless persons to local charities inaccurately assume the level of social services and the manner in which they are provided is adequate for the entire street-involved population. Chapter four shows that EPS officers do not limit their police efforts to aggressive panhandlers as they claim, but instead target homeless-looking persons regardless of their behaviour. Chapter five challenges police officers' attempts to remove the homeless from certain areas through informal move-outs. Chapter six discusses the mobility patterns police agents impose on homeless persons and how these patterns perpetuate the policing of homelessness.

The Production of the Proletariat Argument

The remaining three major scholarly arguments about anti-homeless efforts align with my skepticism of claims that crime prevention alone motivates the policing of homelessness. Todd Gordon (2006, 2010) sets out the first of these positions and contends that anti-panhandling laws do not simply protect the public from crime, but instead seek to maintain the police force's historical function of producing wage labourers. His production of the proletariat argument contends that anti-homeless ordinances like Ontario's Safe Streets Act (1999) resurrect vagrancy laws that criminalize people who try "to find income independent of the market" (Gordon, 2006, p. 90).

Gordon (2006, 2010) maintains that understanding the history of policing and its function as a coercive arm of capitalist society is necessary to analyzing the contemporary policing of homelessness. Following Mark Neocleous (2000), Gordon contends that the central task of the modern urban police force was to aid capitalism's development through the enforcement of vagrancy laws. Early vagrancy laws created the working class necessary for capitalist exploitation by outlawing alternative subsistence strategies like begging and by restricting the migration of poor homeless labourers (Chambliss, 1964; Foote, 1956; Gordon, 2006; Ranasinghe, 2010). Police afforded the deserving poor charity, but used vagrancy provisions to criminalize the able-bodied unemployed and forced them into workhouses where they were indoctrinated with the work ethic required of future wage labourers (Chambliss, 1964; Gordon, 2006; Neocleous, 2000). Based on this history, Gordon (2006, 2010) contends policing always functions to enforce capitalism's ruling relations. As such, he argues that current anti-panhandling laws operate within this same agenda. Although the Canadian Charter of Rights and Freedoms (1982) eliminated vagrancy laws and pushed provisions prohibiting informal economic activity into provincial law and municipal bylaws (Gordon, 2006; Ranasinghe, 2010), Gordon (2006, p. 6) maintains that the "aim of these laws, like the former vagrancy statutes, has been to target behaviour that potentially undermines peoples' dependence on market relations to survive."

Thus, according to Gordon (2006, 2010), anti-panhandling ordinances, like all policing, produce an easily exploited proletariat. Gordon points out that the public safety threat posed by panhandling is poorly established and so argues that the act itself is not the issue that draws police attention (see also Pratt, Gau & Franklin, 2011). Rather, he argues, it is the ability to earn income from panhandling and the fact that panhandlers "consciously try to avoid the drudgery of wage work" that leads to the development and enforcement of anti-panhandling laws (Gordon, 2010, p. 38; see also Gordon, 2006, p. 40). Laws prohibiting informal economic activity or punishing the lifestyles of homeless persons ensure that there are no alternatives to wage labour. In so doing, these laws protect business interests by producing a proletarian army that must accept low-wage work with few benefits (Gordon, 2006, 2010).

For Gordon the fact that current anti-homeless ordinances resurrect vagrancy provisions is the key to challenging these laws. Although the functional and historical link Gordon makes between policing and capitalism suggests that revolutionizing the relations of production and challenging the state's use of police power are the ultimate solutions, he stresses legal reforms. He criticizes laws like Ontario's Safe Streets Act (1999) by proclaiming that they recreate status-based offences and therefore contravene the Charter of Rights and Freedoms (Gordon, 2006; see also Martin, 2002; Schaefer, 2007).

Despite drawing extensively on Neocleous (2000), Gordon (2006) explicitly separates himself from scholars who link police power to agents beyond the state. Consequently, he does not engage diverted giving campaigns, which are commonly led by non-state agents. Nonetheless, there are connections between the production of the proletariat argument and the limited literature on diverted giving campaigns. In particular, Hermer (2001) suggests that diverted giving campaigns help produce proletarians by pushing the homeless into charitable agencies that aim to indoctrinate them with the self-discipline and market rationalities required of wage labourers.

Gordon (2006, 2010) and Hermer (2001) outline a politics behind anti-homeless ordinances and diverted giving campaigns, but they do not underpin their arguments with an examination of homeless persons' daily lives. As such, they leave several questions unattended. What relations do the homeless hold to paid work? Does the employment status of the street-involved figure prominently in the way they are policed? How is wage labour imposed on the homeless persons who draw police attention, if at all? Early vagrancy laws imposed a work ethic on persons by confining them to workhouses, but current anti-panhandling laws do not have recourse to institutions of forced labour (Feldman, 2004). In fact, Edmonton City Administration chose to deny all persons who received anti-panhandling tickets opportunities to pay fines through community service because they felt very few of the those charged would show up to work (Anderson, 2009). Are there other differences between current anti-homeless ordinances and prior vagrancy laws that unsettle Gordon's argument that the policing of homelessness is best understood as a resurrection of vagrancy offences? How does the policing of homelessness continue to protect capitalism, if at all?

The following chapters attend to these questions. Chapter four focuses on homeless persons' encounters with police officers and shows that homeless persons draw police attention because of their appearance in consumer spaces, not because of their relations to wage labour. Chapters five and six discuss how the policing of homelessness continues to promote the interests of businesses. They show, however, that these interests are protected through the creation of spaces and mobility patterns that promote consumerism, not through the production of an easily exploited proletarian army.

The Civic Sanitation Argument

My assertion that anti-homeless ordinances promote business interests by redeveloping space and promoting consumerism shares affinities with the third major scholarly claim about anti-homeless efforts, which Hermer (1997, p. 171) aptly calls the "civic sanitation" argument. Caleb Foote (1956, p. 614) initially used the term "civic sanitation" to describe vagrancy-type law "as a 'clean-up' measure [where] …drunkards, panhandlers, gamblers, peddlers or paupers are committed or banished … to deter other like persons from entering or remaining in a given locality."

More recently, scholars like Berti and Sommers (2010), Damian Collins and Nicholas Blomley (2003), Leonard Feldman (2004), Janet Mosher (2002), Mitchell (1997, 2004), and O'Grady, Gaetz and Buccieri (2011) have revived this position. They contend that current anti-homeless laws do not prevent crime, but instead remove homeless persons from consumer spaces in order to attract tourists, consumers, and investment. O'Grady, Gaetz, and Buccieri (2011, p. 14 – emphasis added), for instance, utilize the language of sanitation when they state that under the Ontario's Safe Streets Act (1999):

> Policing practices to 'rid' the city of visibly marginal persons become justified as necessary to the broader strategy of *sanitizing* modern cities; to help engender a much more positive image of the city and its 'citizens,' thus attracting industry, capital and creative persons in an increasingly competitive global market.

According to the civic sanitation argument, the policing of homelessness sorts out who belongs in consumer spaces and who does not (O'Grady, Gaetz & Buccieri, 2011). In Feldman's (2004, p. 30) words, "anti-homeless laws protect (through exclusion) a consumptive public from threats to its security." For Mitchell (1997, p. 305), this exclusion is so severe that he proclaims anti-homeless ordinances "seek simply to annihilate homeless people." In fact, the severe degree to which many scholars proclaim anti-homeless laws expel the homeless from public space has led Nicholas Blomley (2011, p. 13) to refer to this body of work as the "purification thesis."

Diverted giving campaigns have also been considered exercises in civic sanitation. According to Hermer (1999, 2001), Feldman (2004), and Marjorie Mayers (2001), public education efforts like Edmonton's HHGS campaign direct their message at passersby, but they also tell panhandlers they do not belong in public. Diverted giving campaigns, they argue, seek to hide the homeless in charitable agencies out of view. If panhandlers are pushed off the streets, those with money can enjoy consumer spaces without having to uncomfortably encounter the poor and thus businesses will ostensibly increase profits and neighbourhoods will attract greater investment. Hermer (1999) and Feldman (2004) further warn that although diverted giving campaigns claim to support social services, the measures are not benevolent because they demonize all panhandlers, make street-involvement look voluntary, and so justify police efforts to remove homeless persons from gentrifying areas.

Removing homeless persons from public spaces is, for those who advance the civic sanitation argument, a gross injustice. Scholars like Mosher (2002), Feldman (2004), Mitchell (1997, 2004), and Dianne Martin (2002) contend that public space ought to be a democratic sphere in which all persons can enter and advance their concerns. As such, scholars who advance the civic sanitation argument contend that that all persons, including those without private property, ought to be welcomed in public space (Mitchell, 1997, 2004; Mitchell & Heynen, 2009). Assuring this welcome typically translates into arguments that anti-homeless ordinances deny the poor protected legal rights that would legitimate their presence in public space (Blomley, 2011; Mitchell, 2004), like the right to security of the person (Blomley, 2011, p. 86), the right to mobility (see Blomley, 2011, p. 86), and the right to free speech (Blomley, 2011, p. 86; McNeil, 2010; Mitchell, 2004; Moon, 2002; Schaefer, 1998, 2007).

The insights of the civic sanitation argument are apparent in the fact that business agents, often concerned that homeless persons keep customers away, have developed most diverted giving campaigns (Hermer, 1999) and have lobbied for anti-homeless ordinances and their enforcement (Berti & Sommers, 2010; Hermer, 1997). Additionally, the enforcement of these laws occurs most often in gentrifying consumer spaces and tourist areas (Beckett & Herbert, 2009; Collins & Blomley, 2003; O'Grady, Gaetz & Buccieri, 2011).

The prominent role businesses play in the policing of homelessness is especially obvious in Edmonton. As discussed in the introductory chapter, Edmonton business groups drove the development of the revised Public Places Bylaw (2009) and the HHGS campaign. In addition, although Edmonton's bylaw covers the entire city, the EPS and the HHGS team highlight the Downtown and Old Strathcona neighbourhoods as particularly important panhandling "hot spots" in which they will focus their policing and education efforts ("Anti-panhandling campaign," 2010; Elanik, 2009; Ibrahim, 2010, p. B3). These areas are important shopping and tourist destinations. City Administration also plans to significantly redevelop both locales into even greater pedestrian-led consumer attractions. The City of Edmonton's (2010a, p. 65) *Capital City Downtown Plan* will "[f]ocus on building outstanding street-oriented retail neighbourhoods and completing the necessary initiatives to attract exciting new businesses along special pedestrian-oriented streets, including [popular panhandling spots like] Jasper Avenue, 101 Street, 104 Street and Rice Howard Way." Meanwhile, the City of Edmonton's (2011, p. 5) *Strathcona Area Redevelopment Plan* aims to "[m]aintain and enforce the comprehensive shopping function of Whyte Avenue [another popular panhandling spot] by maintaining pedestrian-oriented retail shopping in the core area and emphasizing retail uses at ground level." Business parties invested in developing areas into beacons of consumerism have thus clearly shaped the development of Edmonton's anti-panhandling efforts and the spaces in which this policing unfolds.

Nonetheless, while the civic sanitation argument helps explain the spaces the policing of homelessness targets, few scholars have examined how that policing is experienced on the ground. As a result, many questions remain. For instance, because the civic sanitation argument derives predominately from analysis of laws and city documents (e.g., Mitchell, 2004; Mosher, 2002), it usually conceptualizes space as city administrators do – as static, gentrifying areas confined by neighbourhood boundaries (Hayward, 2004; Wardhaugh, 1996; Wardhaugh & Jones, 1999). Space, however, is not simply a bounded physical entity but is also socially constructed and given meaning by different actors (Hayward, 2004; Mitchell, 2004). Research on homeless persons' everyday routines demonstrates that the homeless construct and experience space largely in dualistic terms (Feldman, 2004; Wardhaugh, 1996; Wardhaugh & Jones, 1999). On the one hand, their lives are shaped by "prime spaces" that include areas of middle-class consumption from which they are often expelled. On the other hand, they are often permitted to be in "marginalized spaces" comprised of impoverished, stigmatized, and crime-ridden areas "untouched by gentrification" (Feldman, 2004, p. 41; see also Wardhaugh, 1996; Wardhaugh & Jones, 1999). A research method that physically or metaphorically follows the homeless as they move between spaces would better capture their experiences of policing and urban space (see Cresswell, 2010; Hayward, 2004; see for e.g., Wardhaugh, 1996). Current articulations of the civic sanitation argument do not follow the homeless and so do not capture how the homeless experience the policing of space. Are the homeless actually expunged from prime spaces? How? Where do they go? How could the experiences of the homeless help us better develop inclusive city spaces?

I use the stories of the homeless to address these questions. Chapter four confirms the centrality of space to the policing of homelessness. However, chapters four and five also demonstrate how prime spaces provide a contrast between homeless persons and consumers. This contrast underpins the appearance-based policing of homelessness. Moreover, chapter five looks beyond prime spaces and documents how homeless persons are displaced to certain marginalized spaces. Chapter six further shows that the this displacement generates mobility patterns between and within prime and marginalized spaces. Chapter three and the concluding chapter provide suggestions that would make city spaces more inclusive by refashioning these spaces to reflect the lived experiences of the street-involved.

The Pedestrianism Position

Nicholas Blomley once advanced the civic sanitation argument (Blomley, 2011; Collins & Blomley, 2003) but has recently developed a new position that highlights how mobility shapes the policing of public space and is used to legitimate anti-homeless ordinances (Blomley, 2007, 2011, 2012). Blomley argues that the policing of public space, including that which occurs under anti-homeless ordinances, utilizes a police logic of "pedestrianism" that enforces mobility among all persons and treats all people and things as potential obstructions that must be ordered to maintain traffic flow.

This pedestrianism position is the fourth and final major argument about anti-homeless efforts. It directly challenges the production of the proletariat and the civic sanitation arguments insofar as it argues against attributing anti-homeless ordinances to the protection of business interests. Blomley (2011) observed that legal challenges to anti-homeless laws, which have been the tangible reform attempts of those behind the production of the proletariat and the civic sanitation arguments, have failed. Courts have upheld anti-homeless ordinances like Ontario's Safe Streets Act (1999) despite arguments that these laws are status offences which infringe on protected rights like free speech. Blomley (2011, 2012) contends that these legal challenges are unsuccessful because the activists and scholars behind them have reduced anti-homeless ordinances to tools of capitalism and gentrification and so have overlooked the independent police logic of pedestrianism that underpins laws dealing with public spaces.

Examining the discourses of municipal planners, legislators, and judges, Blomley shows how persons who defend anti-panhandling laws and other anti-homeless ordinances employ a police logic that concerns itself with the disposition of things in accord with their overall purpose for the good of society (see also Foucault, 1991; Neocleous, 2000). Blomley demonstrates that this logic argues that the overall function of public spaces like the sidewalk is to enable all citizens to get from point A to point B, not to enable the exercise of individual rights (see also Feldman, 2004, p. 44). When authorities employ this police logic of pedestrianism they legitimate anti-homeless efforts insofar as the police actions behind these efforts ostensibly operate for the good of all by removing obstructions so that all persons can enjoy public space for its alleged intended purpose: movement (Blomley, 2007, 2011, 2012). The police logic of pedestrianism sidesteps rights-based challenges because it frames the debate in terms of ordering things in space so as to ensure mobility. Indeed, this focus on ordering things in space, which is a traffic concern that falls within the jurisdiction of provinces and cities, is why new anti-homeless ordinances appear in provincial laws or municipal bylaws (Blomley, 2011).

Blomley (2007, 2011, 2012) further contends that the police logic of pedestrianism is effective at dodging legal challenges because it presents itself as apolitical by reducing people to things and operating in ways that make all things, regardless of status, potential obstructions. Blomley shows that persons who support anti-panhandling laws use concerns over mobility to equate panhandlers to other potential obstacles on sidewalks, such as newsstands and bus stops, which cities legitimately regulate. In so doing, the police logic of pedestrianism easily trumps individual rights-based claims by arguing that everyone is subject to enforced mobility so that all people can move through public spaces unimpeded. In fact, according to Blomley (2011, p. 32), under the logic of pedestrianism "[m]oral or sociological distinctions are seemingly bracketed" and the panhandler, the transit user, the consumer, and the business owner setting up a sidewalk cafe "are placed on the same evaluative plane" and equally policed as potentially obstructive objects.

Despite the fact that anti-panhandling measures initially put him on to the topic of pedestrianism, Blomley is reluctant to outline the politics of pedestrianism. He explicitly opts to be descriptive rather than explanatory in order to illuminate the police logic of pedestrianism writ large (Blomley, 2011, ch. 9). In Blomley's (2011, p. 15) view, although pedestrianism's concerns over mobility can be used to target the homeless, it is a logic that operates on a principle of equality where all persons and things are subject to enforced movement and legitimately ordered in space to ensure free passage. His central concern is that challenges to laws that order city space will remain unsuccessful until scholars and activists wrestle with pedestrianism as an independent logic with its own organizing principles and discursive maneuvers. As such, according to Blomley (2011, p. 11), linking pedestrianism, even as it operates in anti-homeless efforts, to a larger politics – such as the commodification of wage labour or the banishment of the poor from consumer spaces – "reduces" it to "exclusionary logics" that leave pedestrianism itself unquestioned.

Blomley importantly sketches how authorities legitimate laws ordering public space, including anti-homeless ordinances, through arguments about mobility and the need to enforce it among all sidewalk users. He is not concerned with how that mobility plays out on the ground through the policing of homelessness or urban space. Examining how the homeless experience the policing of urban space, however, raises several questions that would further develop his analysis. Do the homeless experience the enforced mobility that stems from the police logic of pedestrianism? How does policing shape their movements? Does the enforcement of mobility unfold in the apolitical ways Blomley suggests? Blomley may not want to identify a politics behind the police logic of pedestrianism writ large, but Gordon (2006, 2010) and Neocleous (2000) observe that policing often has ties to the interests of the powerful. Additionally, the "mobility turn" (Hannam, Sheller & Urry, 2006) in the social sciences demonstrates the importance of tracing the "politics of mobility" (Cresswell, 2006, 2010, 2012; Hannam, Sheller & Urry, 2006). Cresswell (2006, 2010, 2012), for instance, argues that mobility is much more than travel from point A to point B and should be analyzed as a lived experience shaped by political processes (see also Hannam, Sheller & Urry, 2006). Blomley (2011) encourages future scholars to consider ways to challenge anti-homeless laws and the police logic of pedestrianism that underpins them. Can tracing the politics of mobility as they play out in the policing of homelessness help develop such a challenge?

Chapter six attends to these questions and to the politics behind the policing of homeless mobility. It builds on Blomley's insightful emphasis on the role of mobility in the policing of homeless by demonstrating how policing demands that homeless persons engage in constant movement within or between prime and marginalized spaces. It then uses the experiences of participants to argue that there is, in fact, a "politics of mobility" (Cresswell, 2006, 2010, 2012; Hannam, Sheller & Urry, 2006) behind this policing that continues to support the interests of business leaders and police agents.

Previous Literature Has Overlooked Racialization

Tracing homeless persons' experiences of policing, and the politics of this policing, however, demands attention to the differences among the homeless population (Hulchanski, Campsie, Chau, Hwang & Paradis, 2009). Existing arguments about anti-homeless ordinances and diverted giving campaigns concentrate largely on official discourses and so seldom discuss important differences in how the homeless experience policing. A particularly glaring omission in the above four arguments about anti-homeless efforts is how the policing of homelessness differs according to racial identity. Specifically, although Aboriginal persons in Canada are highly overrepresented in Canada's homelessness statistics (Belanger, Weasel Head, & Awosoga, 2012; Hulchanski, Campsie, Chau, Hwang & Paradis, 2009; Lenon, 2000) and criminal justice system (Samuelson & Monture-Angus, 2002), scholars have paid little attention to the connection between Aboriginality and anti-homeless efforts.

To be sure, Steve Herbert and Elizabeth Brown (2006), alongside O'Grady, Gaetz and Buccieri (2011), note that persons of non-White racial identity are more likely to be homeless and so are more often subject to the policing of homelessness. This observation, however, demonstrates that homelessness is raced. It does not highlight how the policing of homelessness is racialized in ways that lead homeless persons with different racial identities to have qualitatively different experiences of policing. To speak of something as racialized is to discuss how it creates and reinforces differences on the basis of race. Racialization, as Comack (2012), Razack (2002a, 2002b), and Goldberg (1993) define it, is about the production of differences along socially-constructed racial lines. Of course, the production of differences according to racial identity is not, in and of itself, a problem because differences can and should be celebrated. However, racialization is problematic and develops into a form of racism when the creation of differences establishes a hierarchy that disadvantages some groups (Comack, 2012). Policing contributes to racialization, and embodies a form of racism, whenever it serves as "one of the projects through which race is interpreted and given meaning" such that "the racialized order of a society is reproduced" (Comack, 2012, p. 60).

Many authors have documented how policing in Canada is racialized. Racial profiling, wherein police officers more readily suspect non-White persons of criminal behaviour, is one well-researched manifestation of how policing perpetuates racial inequality (Comack, 2012; James, 2002; Tanner, 2009). Racialized policing, however, has many manifestations that extend beyond the discretionary first-contact of individual officers (Comack, 2012). For instance, Comack (2012), Renisa Mawani (2002, 2012), Gordon (2006), and Amanda Nettlebeck and Russell Samandych (2010) separately document how policing contributes to racialization whenever colonial states use police forces (such as the North West Mounted Police) to settle regions and dominate those presumed racially inferior. Comack (2012) further shows that policing contributes to racialization when officers view areas in which people of certain racial identities disproportionately live as dangerous and so patrol them more frequently. Additionally, racialized policing is strikingly apparent when police remove persons of a perceived race out of particular spaces as they did in the infamous "Starlight Tours" that claimed the lives of several Aboriginal males in Saskatoon, Saskatchewan, Canada (Comack, 2012).

The above examples demonstrate how policing helps construct and control Aboriginal persons, yet Cynthia Levine-Rasky (2002) reminds scholars that the category "White" is also socially produced. Consequently, it is pertinent to consider how policing maintains and produces White privilege in the same moment it differentially addresses non-White or Aboriginal persons. In this vein, several authors have documented how police agents control access to specific spaces in ways that restrict Aboriginal peoples to specific locations in order to allow White settlement and domination (Comack, 2012; Goldberg, 1993; Razack, 2002a, 2002b; Mawani, 2002, 2012). Certain spaces are more likely to be constituted as marginalized – or in Razack's (2002a, 2002b) terms as "degenerate" – and certain (minority) races are more likely to be concentrated in these spaces

(Comack, 2012; Herbert & Brown, 2006; Hogeveen & Freistadt, 2013; Mawani, 2002, 2012; Razack, 2002a; Wacquant, 2008).[5] In particular, policing and other colonial processes in Canada have confined Aboriginal peoples to marginalized spaces such as the Reserve, the inner-city, the Residential School, or the prostitution-laden "Stroll" (Comack, 2012; Razack, 2002a; Mawani, 2002, 2005, 2012). According to Razack (2002a, 2002b) policing truncates the mobility of Aboriginal persons and confines them to these disadvantaged spaces, while White persons have their privileged racial identities reaffirmed through their ability to easily avoid these marginalized spaces or freely move in and out spaces as they see fit (see also Mawani, 2002, 2005, 2012).

The scholarship that documents the ways policing and space in Canada are racialized is thus extensive, yet the existing arguments about the policing of homelessness have yet to explore these same themes. Indeed, even though Gordon (2006) describes how policing in Canada has served the interests of capital by first helping exploit Aboriginal people and now by policing immigration, he does not apply his analyses of racialization to the anti-homeless ordinances he considers. Rather, his discussion of Aboriginality and policing revolves around the exploitation of Aboriginal peoples during the creation of the Canadian "White settler state" (Gordon, 2006, p. 33). Renisa Mawani and David Sealy (2011), however, remind us that the colonial processes Gordon (2006) and others document are not simply things of the past. Rather, colonialism mutates and continues into the present (see also Samuelson & Monture-Angus, 2002). Its current manifestations ought to be teased out. How do homeless persons of different racial identity experience policing? How do colonial controls over space and race continue to manifest themselves in the current policing of homelessness, if at all?

Examining how homelessness and the policing thereof are experienced in different ways by persons of White and Aboriginal racial identity helps address these questions. Throughout this book, but particularly in chapter two, I attend to some of the unique factors in Aboriginal persons' lives that lead to their overrepresentation among the homeless and the criminalized. Chapters five and six use the stories of the homeless to illuminate how racial identities intersect with the policing of city space. This discussion brings together literature on the policing of homelessness and scholarship on racialized policing in ways that contribute to both fields. Specifically, chapter five documents how police practices of displacement, and the spaces to which this displacement occurs, are racialized such that Aboriginal

---

[5] I use the term "marginalized spaces" throughout this book in order to link this literature with scholarship on homelessness and to highlight that the spaces are stigmatized and disadvantaged through political processes.

homeless persons are more readily sent to the jail or the inner-city. Chapter six further documents how policing causes Aboriginal homeless persons to endure different and more dangerous patterns of mobility as they constantly return from marginalized spaces to prime spaces. Moreover, it discusses how mobility is not simply a manifestation of power (cf. Razack, 2002a, 2002b) and it documents how the policing that produces racialized mobility patterns among the homeless resembles older colonial controls.

Intervention: In-Situ Interviews with the Visibly Homeless

This book thus contributes to existing scholarship on the policing of homelessness by focusing on the lived experiences of homeless persons. This starting point asks several important questions and can help determine what the policing of homelessness does on the ground, what arguments about anti-homeless efforts reflect the lived experiences of homeless persons, whether the claims used to support anti-panhandling and other anti-homeless measures are accurate, whose interests police responses toward the homeless protect, and how experiences of the policing of homelessness intersect with racial identity. Capturing the experiences of other persons in their entirety is impossible because a researcher cannot become another individual, but it is possible to move toward increased understanding of other people's experiences if a researcher shares in part of their lifeworld and actively listens to their stories (Freistadt, 2011). It is particularly important that scholars help "to 'break the silence' and 'bear witness' to the lived experiences of people of colour and other minorities [like the homeless] in the face of a hegemonic culture that distorts, stereotypes, and marginalizes that experience."" (Henry & Tator, 2006, p. 119 – quoted in Comack, 2012, pp. 160-161).

To this end, I held 22 in-situ interviews with street-involved adults over the spring and summer of 2011. I predominately collected interviews in the same areas the Edmonton Police and the Integrated Panhandling Unit identified as popular panhandling areas: Old Strathcona and Downtown (Elanik, 2009; Ibrahim, 2010, p. B3). However, two interviews occurred in shopping areas on the south side of Edmonton where persons asked me for money or where I often saw people asking for money as I travelled to and from Old Strathcona and Downtown. I went to these field sites two to three times a week from May 2011 through September 2011 and, following Stephen Lankenau (1999a, 1999b), I switched the days of the week I went so that my data would capture weekly variations in the street population. The majority of interviews took place in the morning and early afternoon in order to access public facilities for food and rest and to ensure the sobriety, meaningful participation, and free and informed consent of participants. Most interviews occurred while sitting on sidewalks, some on the grass in parks, a few while sharing meals or coffee in restaurants. In some cases research participants continued to panhandle or vend newspapers while we spoke. Collecting interviews in-situ allowed me to log observations about street life. The primary data for my analyses, however, comprise the narratives of the homeless persons I interviewed.

Interviews aimed to document how Edmonton's revised Public Places Bylaw, HHGS campaign, and other policing measures shaped the everyday lives of homeless persons. William Miller and Benjamin Crabtree (2004) argue that in-depth interviews with open-ended questions that elicit narratives, rather than yes or no answers, can convey the experiences and viewpoints of participants (see also Lindseth & Norberg, 2004; Wimpenny & Gass, 2000). As such, I used a semi-structured interview schedule that contained questions and probes that encouraged participants to provide stories and examples instead of straightforward answers. Questions focused on (i) anti-panhandling initiatives, (ii) interactions with business owners, passersby, police and security officers, and other street-involved people, (iii) the spaces in which homeless persons found themselves, (iv) their use of social services, (v) their pathways to the street, and (vi) their hopes and needs for the future.

I approached persons who looked visibly homeless and were in public spaces. During my first field excursion one street-involved adult was suspicious of my presence on the street. She initially thought I wanted to purchase drugs. Consequently, I decided to make it apparent that I was a researcher and wore the same University of Alberta apparel to the field during every visit. These obvious markers helped me establish familiarity and rapport among the street-involved. By the end of the summer, several participants knew me by name and on two occasions individuals I had not yet formally met identified me as the "homeless researcher" and approached me to volunteer for interviews. Overall, once people were aware that I was a researcher obtaining interviews was relatively easy. Lankenau (1999a, 199b) similarly found homeless persons very willing to tell to their stories. In fact, many homeless people find it "a relief" to talk openly about their experiences to persons from outside the institutions used to manage them (Kraus & Graves, 2002, p. 4).

In addition to homeless persons' eagerness to tell their stories, three key actions improved my ability to secure interviews and ensure quality data. First, I was familiar with this population and employed an "active interview" style that revealed my sympathies (Holstein & Gubrium, 1995). Prior to starting my fieldwork I volunteered at an adult drop-in centre where my primary job was to socialize with homeless and vulnerable clients. This experience introduced me to many of the issues homeless persons face, acquainted me with the vocabulary used among the population, and provided me the confidence to approach and converse with strangers. It also demonstrated to me that my status as a White male student would not dramatically hinder my ability to collect interviews. In the drop-in center, and on the streets during fieldwork, marginalized individuals seemed sympathetic to my research needs because many assumed I too often struggled to make ends meet. They wanted to help. As a White male graduate student I was taken seriously as a scholar and treated with respect, which contrasts with the experiences of some female researchers who found some homeless men held sexist and racist attitudes that complicated data collection (Melrose, 1999).

Above all, however, my interactions in the drop-in center taught me the importance of being honest and empathetic in my discussions. I did not, therefore, try to appear detached from what participants said during my research interviews. I actively responded to participants' stories with sympathy and emotion. In some cases I told participants I shared their disgust and disappointment with how others treated them. If asked, I shared my emerging critique of anti-homeless efforts. In a few cases, participants and I cried together about past traumas. If interviews became distressing, I reminded participants that we did not have to continue and I offered to take them to counselling or services of their choice. None of the participants, however, opted to end the interview or seek aid.

While my reactions to participants' stories inevitably shaped the interview, this shaping did not "bias" the data. Rather, "active interviewing" reflects the interactional nature of all conversation and can improve the reliability of researcher's interpretations because it provides research participants an opportunity to discuss whether they hold similar opinions or feel the interviewer's reactions are warranted (Holstein & Gubrium, 1995). Active interviewing also allows researchers to rely "on the same indicators that are commonly used in everyday interaction to assess the reliability of the information" (Beckett & Herbert, 2009, p. 108). Researchers can change questioning in order to check the internal consistency of stories, assess if the content of a story and the demeanour of the narrator align, and compare individuals' stories with data collected from other sources and participants (Beckett & Herbert, 2009, p. 107). I am confident that my data reflect the experiences of participants based on the emotional vibrancy with which they answered questions and the fact that I heard similar stories from several individuals. Extended time in the field also allowed me to occasionally follow up with participants to corroborate facts.

The second action I took to aid data collection was that I ensured participants' comfort throughout the interview process. During and after interviews I offered the persons I spoke with food, cigarettes, and money. However, following Margaret Melrose (1999), I reduced the coercive effect providing these things might have on homeless people's participation by not telling participants about these provisions until after they had indicated that they were interested in talking with me. The comforts provided were not so large that they would affect free and informed consent. For instance, each participant received \$20 at the end of the interview, which typically lasted an hour. This amount approximates the payment given by other scholars who interviewed homeless persons (O'Grady, Gaetz, Buccieri, 2011, p. 18; Beckett & Herbert 2009, p. 106) and roughly coincides with the hourly amount required to pay a living wage to someone residing in the same city (Edmonton Social Planning Council, 2009). By offering an amount that approximated what a person would be paid for their time if they made a living wage, the compensation offered was fair yet was not so lucrative that impoverished individuals would have trouble turning the money down and not participating. Despite these precautions, two individuals repeatedly asked about the payment during our interview and so indicated that their primary purpose in talking with me was to collect money. In these cases I ended the interviews early because the funds seemed to influence the participants' ongoing free consent. Overall, however, the comforts offered kept individuals engaged and we spoke long enough to cover all the themes in the interview guide.

The final measure I took to ensure quality data involved maintaining the confidentiality of all participants as much as possible. I explained to participants that all publications would use pseudonyms and remove identifying markers (such as the names of specific places and programs). After hearing this, all participants consented to having their interview audio recorded. Holding interviews in public spaces, however, meant that other persons were present and thus the confidentiality of participants during the interview itself was impossible to guarantee. It was not apparent that other individuals in these spaces were eavesdropping and most simply continued to move by and therefore could not hear what was said. Regardless, the presence of strangers did not appear to affect the data as participants continued to share intimate details about their lives. In two cases interviews were held with two street-involved persons who were not strangers but rather well-known partners. These couples wanted to be interviewed together and consented to the interview in the presence of the other person. Again, the presence of the other person did not seem to limit the data. Rather, the couples knew one another intimately and openly shared their experiences. In fact, the couples often shared the same stories and so corroborated individual accounts. The confidentiality and conditions of the interviews thus ensured that individuals were willing to divulge personal details. Indeed, all participants talked openly about sensitive personal matters such as past traumas, drug use, and criminal activity.

Interviews were analyzed using inductive and deductive coding (Berg, 2004; Fereday & Muir-Cochrane, 2006; Hychner, 1985; Lindseth & Norberg, 2004). During deductive coding I applied pre-established codes that reflected my general research question concerning how the homeless experience policing, that stemmed from arguments in existing literature, and that assessed claims used by those who developed Edmonton's anti-panhandling efforts (see Fereday & Muir-Cochrane, 2006; Miller & Crabtree, 2004). For instance, these codes dealt with central themes such as: encounters with police agents, happenings with passersby, the manners in which individuals requested aid, use of social services, locations of events, movements within the city, and opinions of Edmonton's anti-panhandling bylaw or diverted giving campaign. Inductive coding entailed line-by-line analyses for emergent themes (Berg, 2004; Fereday & Muir-Cochrane, 2006). In many cases the inductive codes refined the broad deductive codes. In other cases unforeseen themes emerged from the data. In cases where a new code developed through inductive analyses, I scanned previous transcripts to find similar instances of the code. A single statement could connect to several related codes. I generated the codes myself and used qualitative analysis software to systematically retrieve them.

Racial Identity as a Reflection of Racialization

The 22 participants in this study comprise a convenience sample of homeless persons in the Old Strathcona, Downtown, South Pointe, and Century Park areas of Edmonton. I approached individuals that I saw engaging in informal economic activities like panhandling, bottling picking, or newspaper vending. I also solicited persons who I repeatedly saw on the street, who looked homeless, and who engaged in activities associated with homelessness like loitering, sleeping in public spaces, or picking cigarette butts. In two cases individuals who were not visibly homeless asked me for money, which led to an interview. This group taps the experiences of the homeless persons who are the focal concern of anti-homeless efforts because participants consisted of individuals who spent most of their time in public spaces when housed residents are present. Additionally, since participants were on the street during the day they are also the individuals who are least likely to utilize the social service agencies diverted giving campaigns promote.

Participants' income-generating strategies varied, yet all held connections to panhandling. Of the 22 participants, 19 said panhandling was a regular part of their subsistence activities. The remaining three participants held ambiguous connections to panhandling. One strictly vended the street news although persons giving him money did not necessarily always take a paper. A second survived off social assistance but frequently accompanied his partner while she panhandled. The third participant often received money from passersby but only picked bottles. This book draws on all these individuals' experiences to critically appraise the policing of homelessness in Edmonton, including the new anti-panhandling efforts like the revised Public Places Bylaw (2009) and diverted giving campaign. This is a well-established practice in the literature. For instance, Berti and Sommers (2010), as well as O'Grady, Gaetz and Buccieri (2011), found it necessary to interview homeless persons who engaged in a variety of informal economic activities in order to appraise measures ostensibly aimed more narrowly at panhandlers. In fact, as chapter four will show, police agents used anti-panhandling efforts to target all visibly homeless persons, not just (aggressive) panhandlers.

The participant group contained both sexes and was divided into three racial categories. Interviewees included sixteen males and six females, while the racial identities of participants included eight Aboriginals, thirteen Whites, and one East Asian. The East Asian individual was male, but the other two racial identities contained both males and females.

I employ Carl James' (2002, p. 304) term "racial identity" because this term describes "the socially constructed identification, categorization, or labelling of individuals by race, typically in terms of skin colour ... and other physical attributes." I categorized persons into racial categories in ways that aligned with the argument that race is not a biologically inherent characteristic but a socially-constructed difference that often draws on arbitrary physical characteristics to subject persons to different conditions and institutions (Blackburn, 2000; Comack, 2012; James, 2002; Goldberg, 1993). In particular, during interviews I initially categorized persons according to physical attributes commonly used to assert racial distinctions but then used individuals' stories to confirm or clarify classifications. Such clarification could happen through self-declaration. For instance, the East Asian participant described himself as such when we first met.

In other instances I corroborated racial classifications through individuals' life stories. In particular, while I would initially (and problematically) consider someone Aboriginal if they had they stereotypical darker hair and skin tone attributed to Aboriginals persons (Blackburn, 2000), I only classified them as Aboriginal if they testified – through, for example, discussions about encounters with colonial institutions such as the Reserve System or Residential school – that they had been racialized as such before. Given the important and long-lasting impact of colonial mechanisms of racialization, persons who had encountered these systems of racial classification readily revealed their Aboriginal identities as they described their personal biography. By contrast, those homeless individuals classified as White include those persons who held stereotypical physical characteristics used to construct this category, like fairer skin tone (Blackburn, 2000), and whose personal biographies did not include any of the well-documented mechanisms used to racialize Aboriginal persons. Their stories revealed the privilege accorded to persons racialized as White because they were not subject to special institutions created for "racialized others" (Levine-Rasky, 2002).

By using the stories of participants as the final means of determining participants' racial identity, my categorizations maintain that race is a socially constructed marker used to differentiate and order groups of people. The homeless persons I identify as Aboriginal or White are individuals whose stories reveal that they have been labelled as such. Racial identity, then, does not simply indicate self-identification, nor does it refer to some obvious inherent biological or physiological characteristic. Rather, the term (and my operationalization of it) reflects the social construction of identity categories that are both imposed on, and adopted by, individuals (James, 2002). Of course, using concepts like "Aboriginal" and "White" is problematic insofar as it reifies what are socially-constructed categories, but is it nonetheless necessary because these constructed categories continue to have real effects in individuals' lives (Levine-Ratsky, 2002). Interestingly, all interviewees who would normally be categorized as White or Aboriginal according to stereotypical physical markers like skin pigment (Blackburn, 2000) told narratives that suggested they had been predominately racialized as such and had come to accept that racial identity. This does not legitimate the use of physical characteristics to construct categories of race, but rather affirms the importance that arbitrary, and socially-selected, physical markers have held in schemes of racialization (Blackburn, 2000). Paying attention to how experiences differ according to the racial identities that participants reflected and accepted, allows for consideration of the lasting effects of these means of differentiating individuals and for documentation of the continued ways individuals are racialized.

Caution, however, must be exercised when generalizing from this research to the larger categories of homeless persons, whether they are White or Aboriginal. Although the proportions of Aboriginal and White homeless persons in this study roughly approximate the proportions of these racial identities found in Edmonton's most recent Homeless Count (Sorensen, 2012), these numbers should not be used for statistical interpretation because it is impossible to gather a representative sample of the homeless. Collecting a representative sample requires knowing the characteristics of the entire population, which is inhibited by the fact that some homeless persons remain hidden, dislike social contact, and avoid heavily policed public spaces (Belanger, Weasel Head, & Awosoga, 2012; O'Grady, Gaetz & Buccieri, 2011, p. 18).

It was thus not my intent to document the representative experience of homeless persons generally, or of homeless Aboriginals and Whites in Edmonton. Rather, I use these participants' stories to develop a new view of homelessness and the racialized policing thereof. I collected data until I was confident I could achieve this goal and until the stories I heard were similar to those of previous participants. Because my analyses rely on a non-representative and non-probabilistic convenience sample, this book mainly employs qualitative descriptors (like "a few," "some," "the majority," or "most") to discuss quantities among participants. Exact numbers are not meaningful in this context, risk being read inaccurately as inferential statistics, and detract from the focus on participants' unique experiences of homelessness and policing. Nevertheless, the arguments set out in this book are meaningful because they reflect the lives of a group of people whose experiences have been ignored by most policy makers and academics.

Conclusion: Overarching Argument and Contributions

Collecting data from the homeless thus provides a significant methodological intervention that contributes in several ways to the literature on the policing of homelessness. The dominant arguments in this literature contend that anti-homeless efforts (i) protect the public from fear-generating and crime-causing homeless persons (broken windows theory), (ii) replicate vagrancy law status-offences that protect capitalism by forcing individuals who reject wage labour to become proletarians (production of the proletariat argument), (iii) promote the interests of business by cleansing public spaces of homeless persons in order to encourage redevelopment and create consumer spaces (civic sanitation argument), and (iv) utilize an ostensibly apolitical police logic of pedestrianism that ensures public spaces operate to ensure free mobility flows from point A to point B (pedestrianism position). These arguments largely rely on discourse analyses of the official documents that support anti-homeless efforts. While discourses help constitute the way we think about and therefore respond to things (Foucault, 1980; Hogeveen & Smandych, 2000, p.146), they alone cannot remove fear-generating homeless persons, produce proletarians, sanitize city spaces, or enforce mobility among all sidewalk users. As I have shown, attention to the experiences and stories of the homeless can help reject, support, or refine these four major arguments by assessing how these arguments unfold in the everyday lives of the persons anti-homeless efforts seek to police.

In particular, sections two and three above have outlined how I will use the stories of homeless persons to contribute to each of the four major arguments. I assess the broken windows theory, the production of the proletariat argument, the civic sanitation argument, and the proletarian position against the experiences of participants. I insert into these arguments concepts from ethnographically-inspired work such as "prime" and "marginalized" spaces (Feldman, 2004; Wardhaugh, 1996; Wardhaugh & Jones, 1999) and "the politics of mobility" (Cresswell, 2006, 2010, 2011).

I also significantly contribute to the literature on the policing of homelessness by documenting the ways this policing is racialized.

The overarching argument this book develops is that the stories of the homeless reveal that anti-panhandling efforts hold problematic assumptions about street life and contribute to a racialized policing of homelessness, space, and mobility. The four main arguments in the literature on the policing of homelessness make different claims about who homeless persons are, why homeless persons are (legitimately or otherwise) policed, the politics behind this policing, and how best to respond to this policing. The overarching argument developed across the following chapters contributes to these debates by highlighting what the lives of the homeless are like (in contrast to how they are constructed in official discourses that support anti-homeless efforts) and by using their stories to demonstrate that the policing of homelessness attempts to remove visible homelessness from consumer spaces in ways that rely on marginalized spaces and create mobility patterns that protect the interests of businesses and police agents while maintaining racial hierarchies. I thus argue that efforts to justify the policing of homelessness do not reflect the lives of participants, that the homeless are policed mainly because of their appearance in consumer spaces (as opposed to their relations to crime or wage labour), and that there is a politics behind this policing that protects powerful interests and cannot be fully understood without attending to racialization. Moreover, by documenting how the homeless experience policing I illuminate new ways they are excluded from public space and so develop suggestions to better attend to these exclusions in fashions that reflect their lives.

This discussion progresses in three phases. First, I interrogate the claims made by those who developed Edmonton's anti-panhandling efforts, which reflect the arguments found among champions of the broken windows theory. This happens in chapters two and three. Chapter two shows the claims of Edmonton's anti-panhandling supporters to be exaggerated and decontextualized. Chapter three documents problems with assertions that the homeless ought to be displaced to charitable agencies. Second, I detail how homeless persons' encounter police agents and use their stories to refine the production of the proletariat, civic sanitation, and pedestrianism arguments. This occurs across chapters four, five and six. Chapter four challenges the production of the proletariat thesis and argues that the stories of participants show that they are policed because they stand out in consumer spaces, not because of their relation to wage labour. Chapter five highlights some of the questions that remain unaddressed in the civic sanitation thesis and documents how homeless persons are displaced from consumer spaces into marginalized and racialized spaces. Chapter six reviews the pedestrianism position and documents how the policing of homelessness creates mobility patterns that are not apolitical but instead perpetuate the interests of business leaders and police agents while helping constitute prime spaces as White spaces. Third, in the concluding chapter I summarize my argument and use my findings to develop suggestions for responding to the policing of homelessness and fashioning more inclusive city spaces.

CHAPTER TWO

CONSTRUCTED AS DANGEROUS: EXAGGERATED AND DECONTEXTUALIZED CLAIMS DEPICT PANHANDLERS AS WEALTHY FRAUDSTERS, CRIMINALS, ADDICTS, AND INTIMIDATORS

Images of the homeless as dangerous persons who generate fright and invite crime underpin anti-homeless efforts (Berti & Sommers, 2010; Feldman, 2004; Parnaby, 2003). For instance, George Kelling and Catherine Coles (1997), in *Fixing Broken Windows*, depict homeless persons as dangerous by suggesting that they are fraudulent and criminal addicts who rely on intimidation to secure money. Specifically, Kelling and Coles (1997, p. 230 – emphasis added) argue that criticisms against anti-homeless ordinances are misguided

> given what we know about the nature of the 'homeless' population and many of those who engage in disorderly behavior on our streets: while some may be passive or benign in their speech and acts, many more are *scam artists, substance abusers* feeding alcohol or drug habits…or have *criminal* records. Furthermore, we know that the speech and behavior of many in this population are *intimidating* and even threatening.

By suggesting that homeless persons are frauds, addicts, criminals, and intimidators, Kelling and Coles (1997) depict the visibly homeless as unworthy of support and in need of punitive law and order responses. Because the "homeless" – which Kelling and Cole put in quotation marks to raise readers' suspicions about the actual housing conditions of street-involved persons – are apparently liars, addicts, and bullies, they ostensibly need to be coercively removed from the streets by police officers.

This chapter introduces the study participants and contrasts their stories with the image of panhandlers as dangerous. I argue Edmonton's anti-panhandling efforts make problematic assumptions about street life and that Edmonton's business leaders, EPS spokespersons, and HHGS officials make exaggerated and decontextualized claims when they depict panhandlers as wealthy fraudsters, criminals, addicts, and intimidators. Many individuals' stories contradict the claims of Edmonton's anti-panhandling supporters, while a few individuals' experiences support views that homeless persons are liars, addicts, and criminals. Overall, participants' stories demonstrate that anti-panhandling supporters overlook the diversity among the street-involved population and the context in which some homeless persons engage in fraud, crime, and drug use. This chapter situates participants' lives within this broader context. It explains why a few individuals might align with the claims of EPS and HHGS officials by documenting some of the pathways individuals take into homelessness and discussing the everyday circumstances of living on the street. This contextualization shows that the demonization of any and all panhandlers mistakenly individualizes larger social issues in order to justify policing responses.

This chapter unfolds in three parts. First, I use publicly available documents and news reports to demonstrate that, like Kelling and Coles (1997), EPS and HHGS authorities predominately depict panhandlers as wealthy fraudsters, criminals, addicts, and/or intimidators that prey on vulnerable persons. Second, I use the stories of participants to show that these claims about panhandlers are exaggerated and decontextualized. I take up each major claim in turn. I provide counter-examples to each claim, highlight the diversity among participants, discuss how larger social factors and the conditions of street life shape the behaviours of homeless persons, and critically engage those few cases that align with the depictions of EPS and HHGS officials. I conclude by highlighting participants' pleas for non-prejudicial treatment. Participants hope to, and should be, treated like housed members of society.

Echoing Kelling and Coles

The public messages of those who supported Edmonton's anti-panhandling bylaw and HHGS campaign depict panhandlers as dangerous persons. Moreover, they do so by relying on the same images as Kelling and Coles (1997). They claim that anti-panhandling efforts are required because panhandlers are wealthy fraudsters, criminals, addicts, and/or intimidators that prey on vulnerable persons. Indeed, claims that panhandlers are wealthy fraudsters living lives of luxury off gullible people are common among police officials (O'Grady & Bright, 2002; Parnaby, 2003). In Edmonton, EPS Inspector Brian Nowlan conveyed this view when he highlighted the case of allegedly housed and wealth panhandler. As he discussed the need for an anti-panhandling bylaw, Nowlan told reporters that he knew one "panhandler regularly working on Jasper Avenue who … earns $400 a day tax-free and lives in a high-rise apartment" (Kent, 2009, p. B3). He then stressed that some other panhandlers are "just swindlers" that are "perfectly healthy and capable of holding down a job" but instead decide to "play on well-meaning people's good intentions" (Hanon, 2009, n.p.).

EPS officials also stressed the fraudulent stories and luxurious lives of panhandlers when they hoped to establish the legitimacy of the HHGS campaign. For example, in the same week that the HHGS campaign kicked off its 2011 summer blitz, the EPS issued a press release in the Edmonton Journal ("Edmonton police," 2011, n.p.) "[w]arning the public to save their pity" when approached by some panhandlers. The EPS stressed the story of one "34-year-old con-man [who] visits stores near work sites dressed in overalls and work boots, and claims his truck and tools have been towed away, and he needs $140 to get them back." The panhandler asks for donations toward the amount needed to get his truck back so he can work, but police declare that residents should keep their money because the man is really a "habitual hustler … raking in close to $1,000 a week with the scam." Through these types of stories, the EPS implies that panhandlers often lie about their poverty and housing conditions to gain easy money from soft-hearted Edmontonians.

Tethering criminality to homelessness is also a common strategy of those who support anti-homeless ordinances (Berti & Sommers, 2010; Gordon, 2006; Parnaby, 2003). Proponents of anti-homeless ordinances echo broken windows claims that homeless persons are criminal themselves or invite serious criminals to take over an area (Berti & Sommers, 2010; Gordon, 2006; Parnaby, 2003; Pratt, Gau & Franklin, 2011). These claims were readily apparent in the development of Edmonton's new measures to police the homeless. When the EPS lobbied city council for an anti-panhandling bylaw, officials told the Community Services Committee that panhandling "significantly impacts public safety" by leading to more disorder and crime (Elanik, 2009, p. 2; see also Pallas, 2008). Debi Anderson, a spokesperson for the HHGS campaign similarly told news reporters that it is "important to convey that giving to a panhandler negatively impacts community safety and enables … crime" (Kent, 2010, n.p.). At other points, supporters of Edmonton's anti-panhandling bylaw and HHGS campaign equated panhandling and criminality. In an EPS community crime update video (EPSVideoOnline, 2011), for example, Sergeant Gary Beaulieu explained that panhandlers "support themselves wholly on either panhandling and/or doing thefts" and another officer told viewers that panhandling is "borderline robbery." The video later showed officers arresting an alleged panhandler after declaring that he has "7 warrants." Business leaders who supported Edmonton's anti-panhandling measures also discursively tied panhandling to criminality. According to one news report, "countless small-business owners in Edmonton" feel like "panhandlers are an infestation ... [who] stand outside... intimidating customers...[o]r ... come inside and steal without fear" (McKeen, 2008, p. B1).

Supporters of anti-panhandling efforts further suggested that drug and alcohol addictions plague panhandlers. The brochures and posters for the HHGS campaign, for instance, tell the public that they should not give money to panhandlers because "[g]iving money to panhandlers may support drug and alcohol addictions" (City of Edmonton, 2010b). Indeed, this is the argument HHGS supporters most frequently voiced against supporting panhandlers (see "Anti-panhandling campaign," 2010; Ibrahim, 2010, p. B3, Jacobs, 2011; Kent, 2009, p. A1; McKeen, 2008, p. B1; Rodrigues, 2010, 2011, 2012). Although the full extent of addictions among panhandlers in Edmonton has not been studied, EPS Constable Olena Fedorovich warned people who give money to panhandlers that "nine times out of ten that money is, unfortunately, going to their addictions" (quoted in Kent, 2008, p. B12). One of the business leaders responsible for piloting the HHGS campaign in Edmonton also boldly claimed, "Many panhandlers are drug addicts looking for money to buy crack cocaine" (Shirley Lowe in Kent, 2009, p. A1).

Supporters of anti-panhandling laws also justify police action by suggesting that all panhandlers use aggression and intimidation to coerce vulnerable persons into giving them money (Glasbeek, 2010; Parnaby, 2003). The EPS frequently took this stance. In its report to city council members titled *Public Safety Concerns Related to Panhandling*, EPS officials declared:

An emerging trend and growing concern of late involves reports of aggressive panhandlers blocking and following people for the purpose of demanding money. These panhandlers use intimidation and will often target people that they perceive as weak and vulnerable. Once given a handout, these panhandlers will frequent a location and wait for the person who has given them money in the past to return. If a person refuses to again give them money, they will often be cursed, spat at or even pursued aggressively as a form of intimidation. (Elanik, 2009, p. 2)

The report went on to state that "the overwhelming consensus is that the majority of citizens in Edmonton are afraid of panhandlers" (Elanik, 2009, p. 2).

In many cases, the argument that panhandlers "target" fearful, "weak and vulnerable" persons utilizes a gendered script that depicts male panhandlers preying on female passersby (Glasbeek, 2010). For example, Brian Gibson, the Edmonton Police Commission Chairman at the time, told the public:

> What we are receiving at the police service are a number of complaints. … Women coming to work in the morning or going home at night and being aggressively pursued for monetary contribution … and they are feeling very unsafe on the streets. ("Council to consider," 2009)

Shirley Lowe, the Executive Director of the Old Strathcona Business Association and once a member of the Integrated Panhandling Unit, similarly stressed that "panhandlers not only alarm customers, they scare staff and make it difficult for women to work alone in area shops" ("Why the boom," 2005, p. A18).

Each of the above claims stresses a negative act of homeless persons in order to construct homelessness and panhandling as individual behavioural problems that are most appropriately solved through policing responses. Painting panhandlers as wealthy fraudsters who ostensibly make more "tax-free" money than most Edmontonians and live high-rise lives of luxury dissolves panhandlers' claims to be in need. As such, this position legitimates the HHGS campaign's argument that direct aid to panhandlers is ill-spent and justifies anti-panhandling bylaws by suggesting that many who seek aid are actually "swindlers" (Nowlan in Hanon, 2009, n.p.). Depicting panhandlers as criminals or signs of disorder that invite further criminality relies on a broken windows theory of policing and so supports efforts to remove homeless persons from public spaces (Berti & Sommers, 2010; Pratt, Gau & Franklin, 2011). Meanwhile, constructing panhandlers as persons who simply waste their money on drugs corroborates the HHGS campaign's position that direct aid is harmful. These statements depict the homeless as irresponsible with money and so suggest that punitive law and order responses are for their own good (Collins & Blomley, 2003). Finally, suggesting that panhandlers prey on vulnerable people, especially women, makes the policing of homelessness look like a chivalrous attempt to protect females from intimidating male panhandlers (Glasbeek, 2010).

Overall, these four main claims work simultaneously to remove sympathy for panhandlers and generate fear of the homeless, thus justifying policing responses like Edmonton's revised Public Places Bylaw (2009) and HHGS campaign. But how do they compare to lives of those on the street?

Are all panhandlers wealthy fraudsters, criminals, addicts, or intimidators? Why might this sometimes be the case?

Challenging and Contextualizing Anti-Panhandling Supporters' Claims

Participants' stories paint a much more complex picture of panhandling and homelessness than the images projected by broken windows theorists, EPS authorities, local business representatives, and HHGS officials. The diversity among the homeless complicates the image of panhandlers as dangerous. Many participants' accounts contradict the claims of those who support the policing of homelessness, while a few cases lend credence to claims that panhandling and homelessness intersect with fraud, criminality, addictions, and intimidation. In all instances, however, the voices of the homeless help contextualize these intersections and show that these issues are not simply shared characteristics of a homogenous class of people, but occasional manifestations of histories and conditions of marginalization.

Not Wealthy Fraudsters

Do panhandlers lie about their conditions to make huge sums of money and live in luxury as the EPS suggests? The simple answer is no. The diversity among participations, however, requires us to break up and contextualize the separate themes of luxury, income, and lying that underpin the depiction of panhandlers as wealthy fraudsters.

Participants unanimously countered Inspector Nowlan's caution that some panhandlers live luxurious housed lives. Half of the homeless persons I interviewed lived mainly in public spaces. They slept in alleyways, city parks, or emergency shelters. One lived with another street-involved friend in a garage. The tenants of the house let both of them stay there without paying rent so long as they kept it clean. The remaining ten individuals had shelter in rooming houses or subsidized apartments in the poorest Edmonton neighbourhoods.

All individuals, including those with housing, lived in poverty. Those with housing panhandled to help pay bills because any other income they received, like social assistance, was insufficient to cover all their living expenses. This is not simply a reflection of poor money management and improper purchases as anti-panhandling supporters suggest (Collins & Blomley, 2003). Rather, the poverty of homeless persons ought to be considered within the context of social welfare restructuring (Beckett & Herbert, 2009; Hulchanski, Campsie, Chau, Hwang & Paradis, 2009; Jordan, 1999; Lenon, 2000; Lyon-Callo, 2000; O'Grady, Gaetz & Buccieri, 2011; Rahimian, Wolch & Koegel, 1992). In particular, despite the fact that income assistance in Alberta has been among the lowest in the country since the 1990s (Edmonton Social Planning Council, April 2009; Harder & Trimble, 2005; Lafrance, 2005), the government continues to claw back social assistance payments if persons make money in the formal economy. The bulk of participants' social assistance cheques, however, often went directly to landlords and left them with minimal funds for utilities, groceries, and entertainment. As such, for the housed but street-involved, participation in the informal economy allowed for additional income to make ends meet.

Stan, for instance, demonstrated how inadequate income assistance contributes to panhandling. He lives in a rooming house and collects $900 a month in social assistance. He explained that this is not enough.

> Uh, through welfare, they pay my rent. I pay $600 rent. I only got $300 for myself. I buy only a little bit of groceries and I buy cigarettes. ... So I only got like $70 left and that is not enough for a whole month. So after that, in a week I am broke and I got no food at home. ... So what do I do now? ... I start panhandling so I can get something to eat.

Darlene, who obtained housing through a local charitable agency, similarly told me that her social assistance goes predominately to her rent. Consequently, she fends for herself by selling the street news or panhandling. She explained: "It is just I am paying what money I have now to rent, out of $1200 they get, I get spending money of $30 ... for the month. So I come out here [to Jasper Avenue] and try to get some." Obviously $30 is not enough for Darlene to meet her other obligations. The housing program helped her with her utility bills for the first three months, but from then on expected her to pay. She claimed that the month I met her, after the housing program took her "entire cheque," she "actually spent [her] utility money" on groceries.

Stories such as Stan's and Darlene's stories were typical of all the persons who were involved in the informal economy and on some form of welfare. Even if they were presently housed, none of the street-involved received sufficient income assistance to ensure a consistent roof over their heads. Inadequate income assistance contributed to participation in the informal economy.

Informal economic activity, however, did not ensure needs were met. Panhandling was not as profitable as EPS officials suggested. The amount of money people earn in the informal economy varies drastically, but most persons use activities like panhandling to make just enough money to meet their next most pressing need (O'Grady & Bright, 2002; Tanner, 2009). As Mike explained, "Basically I ask to make enough for a certain price and then I go to the candy store [liquor store]." Mike did not panhandle to accumulate vast sums of cash. Rather, like all the panhandlers in this study, he only worked the informal economy until he had enough money for what he wanted or needed next, in this case alcohol. Panhandler's daily incomes thus reflected the amount they felt they needed to subsist for the day. In Edmonton, similar to William O'Grady and Robert Bright's (2002) findings in Toronto, homeless persons typically earned $40 a day.

To be sure, some participants had stronger needs or wants and therefore reported occasionally making the high sums of money EPS spokespersons highlighted. In particular, because addictions continually demand satisfaction, substance-dependent persons panhandle more frequently and so make the most money (O'Grady & Bright, 2002). The few participants with crack addictions, for instance, said they sometimes made and spent huge sums of money in a day. They panhandled constantly throughout the day in order to continually purchase hits of crack that would satisfy them for only a few minutes. After the euphoria of the high wore off, their craving would be stronger and they would go out again to seek money and drugs. Stan explained:

> I used to smoke crack. I was broke in 5 hours, a thousand bucks. One crack hoot is 5 bucks. You take a hoot and you are in paradise for 20 seconds. Like wow, this feels so good for twenty seconds. That is $5. So you have another one, another one. You could smoke about 200 or 100 bucks in half an hour.

Tina confirmed this experience and reported that she made considerable money panhandling on the days she smoked crack. She said, "It is really stupid when you are addicted to crack-cocaine. I could make $1,000 a day and I would end up with not even a cigarette."

Although Tina and Stan reported making considerable amounts of money when they were feeding their addictions, supporters of anti-panhandling ordinances mislead the public when they use these high amounts to depict panhandling as a lucrative activity used to secure shelter in extravagant high-rises. In fact, individuals who received these considerable daily sums of money did so inconsistently. When they did make large amounts they worked incredibly long hours and never used the cash to sustain a life of comfort. Rather, all panhandlers lived in poverty and found asking for money uncomfortable. Eli, for example, explained that while panhandling, "you feel bad ... and you feel like you are degraded." This humiliation likely contributed to the reason many only panhandled to survive. Those participants with pressing needs or addictions, however, could not let pride get in the way of their cravings. As Nick, a former cocaine addict puts it, "You do not control the drugs, the drugs control you." The addictions of Stan, Tina, Eli, Nick, and others forced them to make these larger amounts of money doing tasks they would not want to do otherwise. These stories of high incomes reflect the dire lives of addicts, not the easy money of panhandling and the luxurious life it affords.

Outside of cases where persons were feeding addictions, profitable panhandling days were very uncommon. Most panhandlers had one story where they made an unusually high amount, but these big paydays were due to large donations from a single individual. Staci's story represents these sorts of transactions.

> Yeah, I was sitting over here and, uh, I wasn't panhandling. I had my cup and all of the sudden this gentleman came up. He says to me, "Here you go." A hundred dollar bill! Of course, I was in shock.

The rarity of these happenings is easily apparent in Staci's surprise. While she has lived on the streets for over five years, this was the only example of a high-paying day she recalled. Rick, who received a similarly large donation, confirmed that it was "just a one-time thing." Outside of this one occasion, he said, "I make a few dollars here day to day and eat to survive. I get by that way." Homeless persons thus might have had the odd day where unusual acts of generosity granted them high earnings, but these days were infrequent. They did not consistently make "$400 a day" as EPS officials have suggested (see Kent, 2009, p. B3). Rather, the money they earned in the informal economy was typically low and they struggled daily to survive.

Additionally, when participants asked persons for money they seldom spun the tales the EPS highlights in its public service announcements. Most panhandlers told the truth about their impoverished conditions or addictions. Many homeless persons felt telling passersby the truth about their lives would help others gain a better understanding of why they were in desperate need. Eli, for instance, softly and sadly told me that that while panhandling "you always, always want to tell people the truth. It is weird." He went on to explain why this was important to him: "I normally do [tell the truth]. ... People tell me, '[Eli] you should just lie sometimes. Tell them a story when you are asking for money.' ... But it's my story, it's true." Like many other homeless persons Eli was ashamed to panhandle, but he was not ashamed to tell his sad story. The story was his and people ought to know about it. It was important to him that passersby understood why he lived a life of desperation. Some other individuals thought that they did not need to tell a story to secure money because their appearance exposed their desperate need. Most panhandlers therefore conveyed to passersby, through their appearance or their story, the reasons they were in need. Very few tried to disguise their dire conditions or utilize "scams." They felt they owned stories that ought to be heard and that hiding their poverty or addictions was pointless.

There was only one obvious exception that confirmed the EPS's claims that some panhandlers lie to receive money. Tina, a self-described "con-artist," always used a fabricated tale to garner donations. Two important factors, however, shaped her situation. First, she did not panhandle in the areas most frequented by the homeless, but in a popular south-side shopping district. Second, she required huge amounts of money because she had a crack addiction and spent most of her nights in motels. She conceptualized her panhandling as a "game" in which she used the same story "all the time" to get "bigger money faster":

I am more of a con artist [laughs]. Like I wheel somebody into a story and, you know. … I find I get bigger money faster. … In this area I run the story for the motel. … "Can you help me out? Like my car broke down. I am not trying to be rude. I am not a bum. … But I have had some troubles. I am trying to obtain a hotel that is across the way, but I am short. I paid for a heavy tow. I have $51 left on me and I am not receiving a money order till midnight. Blah, blah, blah. They won't hold the room. It's cash only without credit. … There is no way I am asking anybody for $26, but if you could help me get closer. I am getting tired, I am hungry."

Tina does not own a car but does use the motel she mentions in her panhandling pitch. Some of the money she makes goes to renting a room there every night. Overall, however, she collected hundreds of dollars a day and spent it as fast as she could make it to feed her addiction.

Although Tina admits to lying and thereby confirms the claim that some panhandlers are fraudulent, her story also provides insights into why this lying occurs. Tina readily admitted to me that she has an addiction. She was not in self-denial. Rather, her story tries to hide her addiction and despair from others in order to receive money. The negative response many people have toward poverty and drug use encouraged Tina to present herself in a different light to garner sympathy. She suggested that her lies were necessary in the affluent area she panhandled:

Here you get that sort of crowd, that pay, believe it, and can afford it. …. You know, rich people will tell poor people to go get a job. Because that is what they did, that is how they obtain it. Or they don't understand it, they just have a silver spoon and they don't understand it. … So the better I look, the better I seem … like brand name, my hair is done, you know? Like today, obviously not this purse, but if I am carrying, you know, D and G [Dolce and Gabana]. And you tell them you are in a one-time situation. Somebody in a one-time situation, these people are more apt to help [because] they can see themselves [in that position]. I tell them "I have a job. I work in [resort town]. Blah, blah, blah. I have a mishap right now. It is taking everything out of me to do this, but I need some help." And they are more apt to help.

Tina's fraudulent narrative thus reflects the fact that some people think the poor and addicted are not worthy of direct aid. She tried repeatedly to disassociate herself from "bums" and to look the part of a middle-class woman who has encountered an unfortunate "one-time situation."

Although most panhandlers told the truth, Tina's explanation of why she uses a fabricated story to secure donations shows that the larger context wherein many individuals demonize addictions and poverty encourages these false tales. When many people, especially those powerful actors who support anti-panhandling efforts, stigmatize joblessness, poverty, and addictions, it should not be surprising that some homeless persons would try to avoid aligning themselves with these labels.

Criminality and Homelessness Have Complex Relationships

The relationship between criminal activity and panhandling also requires contextualization. Participants' stories show that equating all homeless people with criminals is as problematic as depicting them as wealthy fraudsters. To be sure, some participants mentioned previous criminal justice involvement. The criminal activities that participants spoke about ranged from murder, to cases of physical abuse, to drug dealing, to minor thefts. While the most severe and violent cases like murder are incredibly uncommon, research consistently shows homeless persons are more likely than housed persons to engage in violent crime, drug dealing, and property crime (Tanner, 2009). Criminality and homelessness, however, intersect in complex ways. The stories of the homeless encourage us to examine these intersections and consider how the informal economy protects some people from crime, how activities associated with homelessness are criminalized, how the precariousness of street-life encourages crime, and how social policy failures produce both criminality and homelessness.

Alternatives to crime. Mitchell Duneier (2001) addresses the first of these considerations when he documents that many homeless individuals help prevent further crime and use the informal economy to distance themselves from criminal activity. Constructing the homeless as criminals or suggesting that the "panhandler is, in effect, the first broken window" that simply invites criminality (Wilson & Kelling, 1982, p. 15) overlooks how some homeless persons use their presence in public spaces to contribute to public safety (Duneier, 2001).

Several participants discussed ways they helped prevent crimes. Debrah and Kyle, for instance, told me that they acted as nighttime security for an automobile dealership.

> Kyle: We look after the trucks and we keep the place clean and stuff like that….
> Debrah: The dealership guy says … "You guys got to get a place, but I don't mind you guys staying here. … Just as long as you look after my trucks. Make sure nobody touches it." … I had to chase one, actually two, people down.

As homeless persons, Debrah and Kyle are often constructed as criminals or signs of disorder that attract criminality. Their informal agreement with the dealership owner, however, demonstrates that do not simply contribute to community decline. Rather, every night they seek to protect commercial property from theft or vandalism.

While few homeless persons take the direct crime prevention role Debrah and Kyle did, many view their involvement in the informal economy as offering themselves an alternative to crime (Duneier, 2001; Gowan, 2009). Bob, for instance, conveyed that panhandling kept him from stealing when the formal economy offered him few other options. He explained that he started panhandling

> just because it was the thing to do … if you are not going to steal and stuff. And at the time there was very little employment. I used to look for work during the day or whatever, get odd day jobs here and there, pan in the evening. …. It was cooler than stealing.

Without stable lives, shelter, and bank accounts, the street-involved require cash-in-hand to meet their pressing daily needs. Informal economic activities offer ways to earn daily cash without resorting to serious criminal activities (Tanner, 2009). As Bob simply puts it, when your skill set means "there [is] very little employment," actions like panhandling, bottle picking, and newspaper vending are "cooler than stealing." Individuals thus construed their involvement in the informal economy as an attempt to avoid crime. For them, panhandling was appealing because it was not the criminal world of "theft" and "borderline robbery" that EPS officials (EPSVideoOnline, 2011) suggested it was.

Criminal because criminalized. Of course, by outlawing most panhandling Edmonton's revised Public Places Bylaw (2009) denies the separation panhandlers make between informal economic activity and the criminal realm. This criminalization, however, points to one of the complex ways homelessness and criminality intersect. Supporters of anti-homeless ordinances emphasize the criminal histories of the homeless. However, when behaviours associated with homelessness are outlawed, claiming that homeless persons are criminal often confuses the temporality of the situation. What is supposed to be taken as evidence that a person is criminal is a result of treating them as criminal in the first place. Thus, when the EPS ties homelessness and criminality together by informing the public that an alleged panhandler has "seven warrants" (EPSVideoOnline, 2011), it should raise further questions. What are those warrants for? How many are due to the criminalization of homelessness in the first place?

Among participants, the majority of the criminal justice contact they described was related to charges associated with their living in public spaces. Five participants received at least one panhandling ticket, four participants reported receiving at least one drinking in public ticket, four at least one open liquor charge, three at least one jaywalking ticket, two received tickets for pushing shopping carts down Whyte Avenue, three at least one trespassing violation, and one person received at least one ticket for loitering. Police officers use all of these infractions to target things that homeless persons do in public space (Hermer, 1997, Mitchell, 2004; O'Grady, Gaetz & Buccieri, 2011). Since being homeless in public space is often made illegal through anti-homeless ordinances, it is unsurprising that homeless people have ties to the criminal justice system. In these instances the anti-homeless ordinances persons are trying to legitimate by depicting the homeless as criminal are, in fact, the reason many homeless persons have ties to the criminal justice system.

The precariousness of the street leads to criminal activity. To be sure, there were other cases where homeless persons became involved in the criminal justice system for activities that were part of the Criminal Code and not the direct result of anti-homeless laws. Nonetheless, many of these actions were also tied to their homelessness. Homelessness sometimes forces people to resort to crime, like theft, to make ends meet (Gaetz & O'Grady, 2002; Tanner, 2009). The second most frequent stories of crime participants discussed related to these efforts to survive. Some individuals reported that they stole to ensure they had food and clothing. Tina, for instance, explained that she sneaks into hotels and pretends she is a customer so she can eat their free continental breakfast. Joseph said he kept himself clothed through "the clothing exchange program" at a local thrift shop. When I naively asked how the program worked, he laughing told me, "Well you just go in there, grab some clothes and you go into the washroom or change room and swap them out. ... It is called the five finger discount." In both of these examples, the participants spoke of their actions as industrious ways to meet basic needs in the face of poverty.

These relatively-minor criminal activities reflect the precariousness of living in poverty and on the streets. It was not, despite what supporters of anti-panhandling laws suggest, the individual "dangerousness" of these homeless persons that led them to participate in these criminal activities. Rather, conditions of poverty and homelessness led these homeless persons to theft as a means of survival. Homeless persons like Tina and Joseph could have avoided these minor property crimes if their material circumstances provided adequate food and shelter.

Much of the personal and violent crime homeless persons were involved in also reflected the precarious conditions of homelessness. Homeless persons face vastly disproportionate rates of victimization (Gaetz, 2004; O'Grady, Gaetz & Buccieri, 2011; Tanner, 2009). Indeed, participants recounted many stories of violent victimization and frequently bore the marks of recent violence on their bodies. They reported that their homelessness led some members of the public and a few police agents to abuse them.

For instance, although participants described their interactions with the public as generally benevolent, passersby, especially if they were intoxicated, occasionally attacked homeless persons. Dean describes one such encounter where he was assaulted as he picked bottles:

> I had one guy, one night, I am just sitting on Whyte Ave, just waiting for the bars to close to go in their bins, and I had a guy come up and knocked me out. He goes, "Oh here I got some change." And I turned around and I got a shot right in the back of the head.

A few other homeless persons recounted similar stories. Many more spoke of occasions where they were verbally assaulted by passersby.

In other instances persons responsible for ensuring public safety attack the homeless or use excessive force against them (O'Grady, Gaetz & Buccieri, 2011). Darlene, for instance, said that security guards beat her and banned her from a mall after they accused her of panhandling.

> I was actually attacked by [a security guard]. I defended myself, and two others came along. They roughed me up and brought me into a holding cell. … And they said I was panhandling. I said I brought this money in, yes I was [panhandling] but off the property.

Darlene had not done anything offensive in the mall, but her panhandling outside off the mall's property drew the attention of security and resulted in a beating.

In a few other cases individuals reported that Edmonton Police officers assaulted them because they were homeless. Staci recounted one such story:

> I was walking along, actually on the path, not on the road, and [a police officer] just took me in, charged me with jaywalking, and beat my head against the wall. I was unconscious. Both my arms were just smashed to smithereens.

Staci said she did not provoke the attack. While officers initially charged her with jaywalking, she explained that she was "on the path, not on the road" and so could not be legitimately charged with that offence. Her story suggested she too was singled out mainly because she was homeless.

Most cases of physical abuse participants reported, however, did not involve passersby or police agents. Rather, they were most often attacked by other street-involved persons. For instance, Eli initially said that the bruises on his face were the result of a car accident, but then tearfully explained that he was beaten because other people from the street sometimes target panhandlers:

> Look at me. Well, you know, I might tell you the truth about what happened to me. I was panhandling and these other people from the street sometimes rip off panhandlers. They seen me getting some money from one guy. One guy gave me 20 bucks, another guy gave me 50, and I couldn't believe it. ... I turn around ... and these guys, I was watching them, but I didn't think they were following me, they got a hold of me and beat me up for my money.

The visibility of informal economic activities makes persons like Eli prime targets for robbers (Gaetz, 2004). Many participants had been beaten, threatened, or robbed by other street-involved persons who did not engage in the informal economy but preyed upon those who did.

Although most participants' stories of physical assault involved other street-involved persons, constructing the homeless as simply criminal – as supporters of anti-homeless ordinances do – overlooks their victimization and creates a false dichotomy between victims and offenders (Brown, 1995; Gaetz, 2004). Homeless persons conveyed the serious consequences that emerge when authorities ignore their vulnerability and treat them first and foremost as criminals. For instance, the most horrific assault reported to me occurred to Debrah the night before our interview. As a poor Aboriginal woman Debrah' story reflects the unfortunate fact that homeless women of her background face unbelievably high rates of violence (Amnesty International, 2009). Her story also conveys how police officers sometimes fail to see homeless and marginalized persons as legitimate victims. Through tears, Debrah and Kyle told me how Debrah was beaten by a local bouncer so severely she had a miscarriage. Despite the severity of the assault the police refused to investigate the matter.

Debrah: This bouncer picked me up and threw me [shows me some of her fresh and extensive injuries]. … I was outside, picking butts. …
Kyle: He grabbed her by the throat and he fucking dragged her. … She thought she was two months pregnant and then the bouncer hit her and dragged her. And she thinks she lost the baby. … We went to try and charge him [the bouncer] – we are not rats – but we tried to charge him, and the cop was like, "[Debrah] we have had so many complaints about you." …
Debrah: Yeah, for real. And yes I lost the baby.

The police felt that since Debrah had been the focus of previous police attention, her current victimization – which was the most brutal of the many stories I heard – was not worth investigating.

When police dismiss homeless individuals' complaints, especially when the remaining interactions they have with police involve charges or abuse (O'Grady, Gaetz & Buccieri, 2011), the homeless do not feel that they can rely on law enforcement to protect them (Berti & Sommers, 2010; Gaetz, 2004). Mistrust between the homeless and police not only excludes many homeless persons from victim services but it also perpetuates further victimization and crime in the lives of the street-involved. Homeless persons seldom report their victimizations to police because, as Debrah's experience attests, they feel police officers will not believe them or take them seriously. In turn, persons who are aware of this can target vulnerable street-involved persons without fear of official police reaction (Gaetz, 2004). Moreover, because they feel they cannot report victimizations to the police, some homeless persons turn to self-protection and vengeance (Gaetz, 2004).

Indeed, the handful of violent stories participants told in which they were recently perpetrators said these events occurred because they were trying to defend their bodies, their families or friends, their territories, or their belongings from other street-involved persons. Dan expressed the message behind these stories when he said, "We are not out to hurt anybody, but if they [other street people] bother us, we protect ourselves. We are not going to let them beat the shit out of us." Keith similarly explained the necessity of self-defense when he told me, "It is dog eat dog out there. If you are not a big dog, you are gonna get whipped." He felt that in this "dog eat dog" context of homelessness, you had to be tough and protect yourself. Both Keith and Dan saw violence as a more accessible means of protection than the police who were unlikely or unwilling to help them.

Crime and violence among the homeless, then, should not be simply attributed to homeless persons' dangerousness. Rather, a context of precariousness and poor police relations in which the street-involved face frequent victimization yet feel they cannot turn to authorities helps explain some of the violent criminal acts among the homeless.

Marginalization underpins both homelessness and criminality. The relationship between homelessness and criminality is made all the more complex by the fact that social policy failures often generate both homelessness and crime. In these cases, homelessness and criminal activity select the same marginalized people (Tanner, 2009). Examining the case of Stan, the participant with the most serious criminal justice contact, helps illuminate how criminality and homelessness both stem from marginalization through a history of trauma, colonialism, and policy failure.

While few participants mentioned recent serious criminal activity, Stan, an Aboriginal man in his forties, held an extensive and violent criminal record that led justice officials to label him a large threat to public safety. During our interview, Stan showed me papers he carries that outline the conditions he faces as part of a peace bond. If Stan breaches any of these conditions he will go back to jail and likely be classified as a dangerous offender. As he laid the papers on the table he explained:

> I have … 67 charges on my record. … [W]hen I went in front of the … judge [for the peace bond], he said, "Look, you have 16 assaults, 2 assault causing, stabbing, four robberies. Blah, blah, blah. If you don't straighten out, the crown prosecutor has a dangerous offender application on file." So they are just waiting for me to commit one more, not summary conviction, indictable, and once I get that indictable, I am in the pen and I am not ever going to get out again.

Stan said the peace bond was "a wakeup call" and that he was trying hard to abide by its conditions by avoiding criminal activity, drugs, and alcohol. Nonetheless, his history of criminal activity was chilling. His stories certainly demonstrated he was a potentially dangerous individual.

Throughout our conversation, however, Stan complicated any effort to use his story to construct all homeless persons as dangerous criminals by casting light on some of the conditions that produce both homelessness and criminality. He explained how he ended up homeless nearly thirty years ago:

> I grew up in a poor family and everybody was an alcoholic, so I had to move out. … [I have been panhandling since] I was 12. … Because my parents drank so much, everybody drank so much, nobody could give me money. I would wear shoes for five years, you know. My socks

would be just rotten. My nails are dirty. That is how it happened. That is how I was ever since I was a kid. I had to panhandle to make money just so I could clean myself. Take a shower, wash my own clothes. But when I was, uh, panhandling when I was a kid, I had so many problems. I was sexually abused and everything and physically abused. I drank alcohol to hide my problems, forget about my problems.

Stan's past traumas have left him with addictions and severe mental health issues. He tells me "I have a psychiatrist and psychologist … [and] I am on … anti-psychotic medication that helps me not to think violent." Unfortunately, if untreated, Stan's mental illness leads to paranoia and violent outbursts. Over the past thirty years, these outbursts have earned him multiple long-term prison sentences.

Stan is not simply a dangerous criminal because he is homeless. Rather, his violent history, criminal involvement, and homelessness reflect colonialism, his previous traumas, his mental health issues, and inadequate social policy response to these circumstances. Aboriginal families damaged by colonialism have high rates of alcoholism and family abuse (Armitage, 1993; Kline, 1992; Minaker & Hogeveen, 2009). The alcoholism and neglect in Stan's family arguably reflects this history. Stan explains that his parents did not look after him when he lived with them on a Reserve. He did not say much about their history, but it is well documented that colonial social policy failures like the Residential School system stripped generations of their ability to parent in traditional ways. In place of traditional family structures and parenting routines, colonialism helped develop frustrated and abusive environments in some Aboriginal homes (Armitage, 1993; Minaker & Hogeveen, 2009). Stan's household was one of these abusive and traumatic environments. As such, he understandably fled to the city streets.

Unfortunately, the day to day precariousness of being homeless makes it difficult for street-involved persons to maintain consistent health regimes (Hwang, 2001). Stan thus struggled to secure treatment for his mental health issues and turned to drugs and alcohol "to hide his problems." This only increased his criminal and violent behaviour. He soon found himself repeatedly integrated into the criminal justice system. The criminal justice system, however, does not adequately address housing or mental health issues (Gowan, 2002; Service, 2010; Thomson, Knutson, deKoning, Grekul & Fawcett, 2010). After each of his jail terms, criminal justice officials repeatedly released Stan, untreated, into homelessness or inadequate housing.

Stan's story confirms the EPS's broken windows position that some homeless persons are dangerous criminals and present public safety threats. Nevertheless, using cases like Stan's to depict all homeless persons as criminal is a problematic exaggeration. Moreover, his life story reveals that equating homelessness and criminality overlooks how larger social factors produce involvement in both the street and the criminal justice system. His story shows the damaging legacy of colonialism (Minaker & Hogeveen, 2009), the homelessness that follows the deinstitutionalization of mental health (Beckett & Herbert, 2009; Rahimian, Wolch & Koegel, 1992), and the criminal justice system's failure to ensure it releases prisoners into positive housing conditions (Gowan, 2002; Thomson, Knutson, deKoning, Grekul & Fawcett, 2010). When supporters of anti-homeless ordinances construct the homeless as criminal, they blame the homeless individual and punish that individual for the policy failures that produce both homelessness and criminality.

Not Simply Feeding Addictions

Painting all panhandlers as addicts is as much a decontextualized and exaggerated image as the idea that panhandlers are criminals. Arguments that giving to panhandlers enables their addictions provide a narrow view of the lives of the street-involved. To be sure, drug and alcohol addictions are vastly overrepresented among the homeless. Addictions can lead to homelessness as they strain family ties, while living on the streets can lead to drug use (Kidd, 2012; Minaker & Hogeveen, 2009; Tanner, 2009). These strong associations between street life and substance abuse, however, should not lead persons to conclude that all homeless persons are current addicts.

In fact, among the participants there was a range of substance abuse issues and histories. Just over half had current addictions. The majority of these struggled with alcoholism, a few with a crack addiction, and one participant did not speak about addictions issues but was anxious to receive the monetary reward I offered. The remaining participants reported that they were not addicted to any substances at the time of our interview. Of these individuals, most had previous drug or alcohol additions but reported being clean for a significant period of time, while only a pair of interviewees claimed that they never abused substances. Of those who said they were now clean and sober, a couple declared that they had been sober for a few years but either relapsed or were dishonest as I later encountered them intoxicated, another had just been released from a three month treatment program a week before we met, one had quit drugs and alcohol on his own after being released from prison three months prior to our meeting, and the others had been clean for several years. Unfortunately, supporters of Edmonton's Public Places Bylaw (2009) and HHGS campaign do not mention that many homeless persons might not be current drug users or that some might have never used drugs. Rather, they suggest that "nine times out of ten" the money panhandlers receive goes to drugs or alcohol (see Constable Fedorovich in Kent, 2008, p. B12). Such claims fail to capture the full diversity of substance issues among the homeless.

Anti-panhandling supporters also mislead the public when they suggest that all money earned in the informal economy goes toward substance abuse. In truth, homeless persons have multiple urgent needs for which they require daily cash (O'Grady & Bright, 2002; Tanner, 2009). Participants, including those with addictions, utilized the incomes they received for many different ends. These included giving money to family and friends, or purchasing food, clothing, hygienic items, cigarettes, transportation, drugs, alcohol, shelter, or telephone access.[6] Drug and alcohol consumption was only one of ways people spent income earned in the informal economy – and that was only for a segment of the homeless population.

In one case an individual, Jason, used the money he initially requested from me to pay outstanding bank fees. Jason insisted that I accompany him to the bank so he could prove he needed the money to keep his account open. After we left the bank, Jason explained that an alcoholic past has left him with short-term memory loss. Consequently, he "do[es] things twenty times a day, over and over" and so often exceeds his transaction limits and has to pay exorbitant fees. He explained that it deeply offends him when people assume that he is a drug user because he is homeless:

> And I hate it when people accuse me of being a crack head. That insults. The worst I ever did is I smoked dope when maybe I was 13 years old, a couple times. But I couldn't stand the junk, have had nothing since then. … Yeah, people figure that since you are on the street you are a crack head. I have never used the stuff in my life, never. I don't drink, I can't stand the smell of alcohol anymore … it makes me sick.

Jason demanded I follow him into the bank because he wanted to shed assumptions that panhandlers are addicts. There are several unfortunate reasons for being homelessness but Jason's reasons, along with many other participants, did not involve current addictions. Jason fought alcoholism and has been clean every since. Assuming that he is still an addict discredits his unique story and denies how, against the odds, he triumphantly turned away from alcohol and refused other drugs.

Even in cases where persons panhandled to support addictions, the argument that giving to panhandlers enables addictions presents an incomplete understanding of the source and power of addictions. Drug and alcohol addictions often reflect efforts to self-medicate trauma, especially

---

[6] See Lankenau (1999b), O'Grady and Bright (2002), and Tanner (2009) for similar findings in other cities.

among the homeless (Klee & Reid, 1998). All of the participants who struggled with addictions had traumatic pasts and often said they used drugs or alcohol to cope with either the harsh realities of street life or the issues that led to homelessness. Staci captured the sentiment among most participants with addictions when she sadly stated, "I would drink to make the pain go away. And it doesn't always go away." For some participants, the conditions of street life and panhandling contributed to substance abuse. Darlene, for example, said she drank heavily to "keep warm" and that she "would have to be half-shot [intoxicated]" to panhandle since "it was embarrassing at first because people would be rude, swear at you, [tell you to] get a job." Demonizing individuals who panhandle to feed addictions overlooks why these individuals have addictions. In some cases, like Darlene's, this demonization itself drives drug and alcohol consumption.

Without adequate treatment, the strength of these addictions meant participants were going to pursue their habits regardless of the availability of donations. Outlawing panhandling or curbing donations ignores the severity of need or addiction among some homeless persons and potentially leads some panhandlers to turn to criminal activities that produce greater harm (O'Grady & Bright, 2002). Participants did not say that they would turn to crime if they could not panhandle, but they speculated that this might be the case for many other panhandlers.

Nick, for instance, criticized the shortsightedness of the HHGS campaign's directive to not give to panhandlers because they are ostensibly addicts:

> I think it is hurting the people that need it. Because I don't care that these guys [other panhandlers in the area] are going to get a bottle. What is going to happen eventually is that they are going to have more stealing, more robberies and so forth. Because these people have nothing.

Nick beat his addiction several years ago but felt that people with addictions "who have nothing" would do anything, including stealing and robbing, to secure drugs. When he was addicted to crack and could not get money panhandling, he had resorted to theft. He felt that individuals with addictions would similarly continue to secure funds to purchase drugs regardless of the availability of direct donations from passersby. He thus points out that campaigns to curb donations to panhandlers will remain ineffective at removing addicted homeless persons from the street because they do not address the addictions that put or keep some persons on the street in the first place.

Politeness and the Panhandlers' Code

Anti-panhandling supporters also depict the homeless as intimidators without considering the accuracy of this image. In fact, of all the claims used to construct panhandlers as dangerous this one received the least credence among participants. The panhandlers in this study unanimously rejected claims that they used intimidation and frightened vulnerable people into giving them money. Rather, they all stressed that they were not causing harm to other individuals. Kelly, for instance, explained, "The homeless are harmless. They don't ... rob people. You know, they just like sleeping anywhere they could possibly sleep. Because when you are homeless, where are you going to sleep?" Eli similarly felt there was no reason to fear him and the other homeless persons he knew. He stated that at times people are "scared of us. I don't know why. I am often not [scary]. We are hurting ourselves mostly, but this is all we live for." Both Kelly and Eli argued that they and others are simply living their lives in public space and are not causing considerable direct harm to other people.

As part of their declaration that they did not cause harm to others, participants stressed that they never relied on intimidation to garner donations. They predominately relied on subtle requests to seek aid. In fact, none of the panhandlers used signs or other measures to draw extra attention and many sought aid in the most passive manner possible by sitting silently in public space. These individuals did not even verbally ask for help. Bob and Jason reported that this passive strategy was more successful than asking passersby for money. Bob explained, "I don't ask. ... I just sit there with a cup because a lot of people get annoyed if you ask." Jason said, "I don't ask, what I do most the time is stick out my hat. Because I found out that if you ask, people almost never ever give you anything. Not even a cent." By sitting quietly and simply letting poverty speak for itself, the behaviour of panhandlers like Bob and Jason was far from the intimidating requests the EPS emphasized.

Several other participants, of course, did ask for passersby's help. However, contrary to claims that panhandlers target and scare vulnerable persons, those who explicitly ask for aid usually abide by an implicit code of conduct that stresses being polite (Dean & Melrose, 1999; Duneier, 2001; Mayers, 2001; Lankenau, 1999a, 1999b) and only approaching people who look unafraid and as though they can afford to spare money (Mayers, 2001; Lankenau, 1999a, 1999b). Participants confirmed that they always tried to be friendly and courteous regardless of how passersby treated them. Eli, for example, reported:

I have never insulted anybody. I have never put down anybody. Somebody swore at me for absolutely no reason because I was asking him if he could spare any change. ... I just went, "Oh, thank you," and I walked away.

Nick went further and took negative responses as opportunities to display politeness and win people over. He said:

One of my challenges ... that keeps me going is when people give me a dirty look, I smile at them. I worked my way through the [business] people, so that people that wouldn't even talk to me will pick me up a coffee now. ... You know, like you are not aggressive with them and it works. And that is not to get a coffee; it is just to prove something to them.

I witnessed many requests for money during my fieldwork and although people sometimes shot panhandlers disturbing looks, all participants reacted in the polite manner discussed by Nick and Eli.

Those panhandlers who explicitly outlined the strategies they used to ask for money also reported that they did not prey on vulnerable persons. Eli, for instance, suggested that panhandlers he knew only asked people who likely had money and would not be scared by the request. He said:

We never ask children, we never ask teenagers, we always ask a man that is over 40s. ... We don't ask young people ... because we respect them and, not only that, they are trying their best to make it.

Vaughn also told me, "I don't usually ask a lot of woman. ... I don't know why. I got a lot of respect for women and I don't feel comfortable asking a lady. ... They don't know what to expect from me [a stranger]." Thus, contrary to the claims of anti-panhandling supporters that panhandlers target easily frightened women, Vaughn declared that he does not ask women because they might get scared. Dean also explained that he does not ask persons who look scared. Rather, he only asks persons who look happy. He said, "With me, if a person is not smiling or they don't look too happy, I won't ask them. But if they look like a happy-go-lucky person, that is a person I will ask."

Participants like Vaughn, Dean, and Eli likely did not ask individuals who looked sacred for money in order to avoid having these persons complain about them to police agents. To be sure, the EPS reports that it receives many complaints about panhandlers from scared passersby (Pallas, 2008). Nevertheless, constructing all panhandlers and homeless persons as intimidating predators that prey on vulnerable persons ignores how most of the street-involved engage strangers.

Conclusion: Homeless Persons Call Everyone to Shed Prejudice

The stories of the homeless complicate broken-windows inspired claims that they are best understood as dangerous. Their stories counter and contextualize the arguments of those who supported Edmonton's newest efforts to police the homeless. Participants showed that Edmonton's anti-panhandling efforts make several problematic assumptions about street life. The diversity of their lives demonstrates the exaggerations among claims that panhandlers are wealthy fraudsters, criminals, addicts, and/or intimidators. Moreover, their stories revealed how larger social factors, stereotypes, colonial histories, relationships with law enforcement, criminalization, and the harsh conditions of street life, influence the few cases that align with these negative depictions of homelessness and panhandling.

All participants lived in poverty and turned to panhandling and the informal economy to try and make ends meet within a disintegrating social safety net. There were a few instances where panhandlers made vast sums of money and used lies to receive this money. These occasions, however, were rare. The incomes of all participants were inconsistent and unreliable. Most participants were honest and made only enough to survive. The exceptional cases that involved big paydays and fraudulent tales reflected the stigmatized lives of impoverished addicts. No one wanted to panhandle. Their addictions and poverty pushed them into this activity, not the allegedly lucrative and easy money that could be had. When broken windows theorists and the EPS emphasize the few panhandlers that lie to make vast amounts of money, they distort the experiences of most of the homeless and fail to question why people might falsify their reasons for panhandling.

Depicting homelessness as criminal similarly exaggerates and decontextualizes the lives of homeless persons. Equating homeless people with criminals ignores the complex relationships between homelessness and crime. It overlooks the criminalization of homelessness, how the conditions of street life push some homeless persons into criminal activity, and how social policy failures often produce both criminality and homelessness. Meanwhile, claims that homelessness is a sign of social disorder that invites other criminals overlook the pro-social behaviours and crime prevention tasks of some homeless persons.

Broken windows theorists and other supporters of Edmonton's HHGS campaign and anti-panhandling bylaw have also exaggerated the presence of current addictions among the homeless while overlooking the diversity of substance issues that befall the homeless. Participants described a range of addictions issues. Some were substance-dependent, some were recovering, some were relapsing into use, and some never had addictions. People behind Edmonton's newest efforts to police the homeless do not fully consider the reasons for, and the strength of, addictions. Moreover, in an effort to paint panhandlers as dangerous addicts in order to advance the Public Places Bylaw (2009) and the HHGS campaign, they fail to see that these policing measures do not address the cause of addictions.

Participants also countered claims that panhandlers rely predominately on intimidation and prey on the vulnerable. All participants described their panhandling as passive and polite. Many outlined an implicit code that stressed being respectful and asking persons who did not look afraid. The EPS claims to receive many complaints about aggressive panhandlers, but no one in this study used intimidation to garner donations. In fact, most found passive forms of panhandling to be far more successful.

"We Are All Human Beings"

The voices of the homeless present a much more complicated picture of street life than the image of dangerous homeless persons constructed by anti-panhandling supporters. Only by ignoring the diversity among the homeless and the context in which their lives unfold can the image of panhandlers as dangerous reign dominant in public consciousness. Participants felt the effects of this negative image. They often pleaded to not be treated as though they were a homogenous category of dangerous people unworthy of occupying public space and worthy of punishment. They did not want to be painted with broad brush strokes.

Joseph, for example, emphatically proclaimed that he deserved to be treated without prejudice:

> I am not saying all, but some… people are… really rude. [They say things like,] "Get the fuck away from me. Don't fucking even come and ask me." … Maybe, you know what, maybe in the past they have had bad experiences with individuals that are outside [homeless]. So they automatically come to the conclusion that everybody that is outside is on something or other, or just stupid, or dangerous, or whatever. And you know, I kind of understand and relate. … [But] you can't totally automatically presume. … Like I [am not] going to hurt nobody. I don't give a fuck what people say. Because you know what, nobody is greater than anybody. We are all human beings. We are all equal. I am pretty sure each every person in here bleeds the same color as I do.

Joseph understood that some people might fear all homeless persons based on a few negative encounters. Like all other participants, however, he did not appreciate the prejudice that comes with this attitude. He exclaimed, "We are all human beings" and hoped people would not simply assume he is dangerous. He wanted to be treated as respectfully as other Edmontonians, housed or otherwise.

Indeed, participants' desires to be treated respectfully, and to not be prejudicially categorized as dangerous simply because they are homeless, must echo throughout all responses to the homeless. The next chapter, for instance, shows that a continued failure to appreciate the individual stories, experiences, differences, and preferences among the homeless has lead many street-involved persons to avoid or resent Edmonton's crises-oriented social services. Their experiences with the street and social services, as I will show, continue to reveal problematic assumptions among those who support Edmonton's anti-panhandling efforts.

CHAPTER THREE

TOLD TO SEEK HELP FROM CHARITIES: REDIRECTING THE HOMELESS TO SERVICE AGENCIES DOES NOT NECESSARILY HELP

"Giving money to panhandlers may discourage them from accessing community resources that help."

"If you **really** want to help people in need, **please support agencies** that provide food, shelter and other resources."

City of Edmonton (2010b) in its "Have a Heart, Give Smart" campaign materials

These opening quotations admonish individuals who feel compelled to help needy strangers. They contend that direct aid harms panhandlers because it dissuades them from accessing local "support agencies" that "really" help. In place of such aid, these claims encourage individuals to send their money and the homeless to local charitable agencies. The HHGS brochure (City of Edmonton, 2010b) stresses that "[t]here are many services and supports available in Edmonton" and points people to an index of organizations that provide food, shelter, skills development, and emergency counselling. According to EPS Constable Dwayne Williams, passersby ought to direct panhandlers to these agencies. In a 2012 press release, he advised readers that instead of giving panhandlers money that will prevent them from seeking agency help, "you could tell them which agency you support and how to find it." A spokesperson from the City of Edmonton Community and Social Development Branch similarly told Edmontonians, "Just say no, and offer them [panhandlers] information" (Rodrigues, 2012).

Although city council endorsed the HHGS campaign as an anti-panhandling response because several citizens and councilpersons were concerned the bylaw alone would be too punitive, Leonard Feldman (2004) cautions against seeing diverted giving campaigns as benevolent alternatives. Rather, he observes that messages that highlight the services available to the homeless often assume that these services, no matter how they are delivered, are adequate and appropriate. He further argues that if people unquestioningly accept that current charitable agencies can resolve homelessness, then they are more likely to see being on the street as a voluntary condition that is justifiably punished through law and order responses. Indeed, broken windows proponents like George Kelling and Catherine Coles (1997, p. 228) have encouraged city administrators hoping to develop anti-homeless ordinances to stress the existence of services for the "poor and indigent." In their view, stressing these services will "dispel the notion that the city intended in any fashion to discriminate against the indigent, homeless, or otherwise disadvantaged persons through its order maintenance efforts" (Kelling & Coles, 1997, p. 228).

The HHGS campaign's message that panhandlers ought to use the services available and Edmonton's revised Public Places Bylaw (2009) thus work together to constitute visible homelessness as a problem of individual lifestyle choices that is legitimately policed. According to this broken windows logic, the homeless do not need to be in public view and should simply help themselves to exiting services. Homeless persons' failure to use these services apparently warrants police action.

This chapter again documents how Edmonton's anti-panhandling efforts make problematic assumptions about street life. I argue that the efforts of police officers and the HHGS campaign to redirect panhandlers to service agencies inappropriately suggest that the level of services and the manner in which they are provided is adequate for the homeless population. Participants' stories document the reasons they avoid many social service agencies. These include inadequate capacity among services, overt dangers in and around facilities, and programming that is out of sync with clients' ideas of themselves self as autonomous consuming adults who often hold caring inter-personal relationships.

The charitable organizations discussed here are predominately crisis-oriented agencies that provide individual counselling, food, and shelter. These are the agencies the HHGS campaign informs the public are available to homeless persons. They include night shelters, soup kitchens, and daytime adult drop-in centres. Additionally, a few housed but street-involved individuals who accessed Housing First programs that offer more intensive supported living (see Klodawsky, 2009) provided insights into these programs and the reasons they remained street-involved while having access to shelter.

My discussion of homeless persons' encounters with charitable agencies unfolds in four parts. First, I discuss participants' ability to access local programs. Second, I demonstrate several dangers around charitable organizations that caused some homeless persons to avoid utilizing their services. Third, I present some of the complaints individuals had about services they utilized and show how these services often misaligned with their aspirations to be autonomous subjects who could purchase their own consumer goods and maintain caring relationships with other persons. I conclude by offering several suggestions that would help social service agencies better reflect the lives of these street entrenched individuals.

Closed Doors and Treatment Gaps

Despite the EPS's and the HHGS campaign's statements that passersby should inform the homeless of the charitable agencies available, all participants were aware of the city's services and did not need to be patronizingly told where to go to secure help. Most homeless persons had used local agencies at least once to sleep, obtain clothing, stay warm, maintain personal hygiene, visit counsellors, secure day labour, detoxify themselves, socialize with friends, obtain food, get help with income assistance forms, or access mail. Nonetheless, all participants preferred not to rely solely on the charitable agencies to meet their needs. Homeless Aboriginals reported more contact with local agencies than their White counterparts. However, since they too preferred not to attend many of these facilities, their more frequent use likely reflects that fact that, as the following chapters show, police were more likely to push Aboriginal homeless persons into the neighbourhoods that contain these services.

It was not, contrary to the HHGS campaign's message, the generosity of passersby that drove many homeless persons away from local agencies. In fact, panhandling did not prevent individuals from using charities and individuals who relied predominately on panhandling used social service agencies more than homeless persons who never or seldom panhandled. Rather, the major obstacles to service use existed among the charitable agencies themselves. In particular, limited capacity to serve the street-involved was the most obvious hurdle to accessing services. Despite the HHGS campaign's declaration that there are "many services and supports available in Edmonton" (City of Edmonton, 2010b), there are simply not enough spaces to meet the needs of the entire homeless or impoverished population in Edmonton.

Participants particularly highlighted a shortage of food services. Steve, for instance, explained his frustration with a local agency that provides free lunches:

> They only allow so many people in their building and you got to sit outside like a dog, waiting until somebody leaves and they let two more in, two leave, two in. I have been down there to try and get a lunch. Well lunch is over by the time I get through the door. ... Before they opened the door and they let people come in and eat. Now it is like you stand there waiting. ... It is just a pile of shit, think about it. ... If you got to rely on that to eat, well that is not good enough.

Steve's description shows how demand for complimentary food now exceeds supply. At one time agencies let everyone in, but now they practice "first come, first served." In this context, Steve felt the agencies treated him "like a dog" begging for dinner only to sometimes send him away empty-handed. He could not rely on the available services for consistent food.

Arguments that panhandlers ought to utilize support agencies for food fail to consider the ability of those agencies to feed the hungry (Gaetz, Tarasuk, Dachner & Kirkpatrick, 2006). In fact, many panhandlers found the informal economy was a more reliable and quicker means of obtaining food. Nick, for instance, said that he too has waited hours in lines at various soup kitchens to "not even get a sandwich sometimes." Since he started panhandling, however, he has "never had to use the food bank or any of those facilities."

Other essential services like emergency shelter were also in short supply. Darlene, for instance, explained that she disagrees with the HHGS campaign's logic that giving donations to panhandlers dissuades them from using the support agencies because "a lot of people are rejected from shelters." The fact that Edmonton agencies repeatedly have to craft additional emergency shelter spaces during the winter corroborates Darlene's claim that current shelter capacity is insufficient (Cormier, 2008, p. B4; Sands, 2009, p. A1; Wittmeier, 2012). Women in particular face a shortage of appropriate or female-only shelter spaces (Goodman, Fels, Glenn & Benitez, 2011; Minaker & Hogeveen, 2009). Darlene confirmed this was the case in Edmonton when she said, "Like, for women, I know there [are] not many facilities for us. There [are] more for men."

Securing services like shelter was further complicated by the constantly changing landscape of social service provision. A few individuals faced prolonged homelessness because the administrative responsibility for programs constantly shifted and the bureaucratic red tape to access programs was thick. Jason, for instance, explained how each time he falls into homelessness, he has to reapply for rent subsidy because the agencies that administer aid change:

> Well the rent subsidy thing, back then it was actually administered by welfare or something. I got approved for it and they put the extra money in my account along with everything else. I used it to get a security deposit to get a place and the first month's rent. Then it quit. The next time, welfare no longer handled it. … [I]t went back to Capital Region Housing. The thing was, in order to get it back I had to re-apply for it. … And in order to apply you have to prove you only have a certain amount of income. For that I need tax receipts, notices of assessment, letters from everybody I can think of saying, "Ok, this is how much he makes a month, this how much he makes from so and so, this is his income from other people. This is where that went." But, yeah, I have to reapply for that.

Jason was homeless because he had to yet again arrange all the cumbersome paperwork to reapply to a program which he was in twice already. At the time of our interview he was still working on his latest application to obtain a rent subsidy. The cycle in and out of homelessness that many people like Jason encounter (May, 2000; Peters, 2012), the continual change in housing administration, and the need to reapply for programming when each new instance of homelessness occurs, burdens people who need housing immediately.

Gaps among services created further obstacles. Fragmented social services produce several gaps that send homeless clients bouncing from one organization to the next (DeVerteuil, 2003; United States General Accounting Office, 2000). When individuals could access some help from charitable agencies, they seldom received the additional or follow-up services they required. This was particularly evident among the agencies that provided addictions recovery. Multiple services must sync for persons to receive full addictions treatment. According to participants this seldom happened. All the addictions treatment programs they knew about in Edmonton required them to first "dry out" in a detoxification centre before finding a treatment bed in another agency. Spaces in detoxification centres were not always available and usually only allowed visitors to stay for limited periods of time. Vaughn described how stays in these centres are typically short-term:

> Detox is 5 days … and then they [workers] kick you out – well you are asked to leave – because people after 5 days [clients] are sobered up and … are ok. So after 5 days they [workers] make more room for other people.

Unfortunately individuals who managed to secure detoxification beds found treatment spaces unavailable when they finish their short stints of "drying out." To meet the large demand and "make room for other people," most homeless persons were sent back to the difficult conditions they were in prior to entering detoxification. They were supposed to maintain sobriety on their own until they could find an appropriate treatment bed.

If homeless persons did make it to a treatment bed, exits from the treatment centre often sent them back to unstable housing conditions. As Eli sadly explained, his departure from addictions treatment was simply, "see you later." Workers did not ensure he went from treatment into suitable housing. It is incredibly difficult for persons with addictions issues to remain sober without supports, especially if they are street-involved (National Coalition for the Homeless, 2009). As such, many homeless persons, including Eli, relapsed back into substance abuse. These individuals fell through gaps in social service provision and hit familiar hard streets.

Given the gaps and shortages in local services, directing the homeless to support agencies is not as straightforward as EPS officials and the HHGS campaign suggest. It is of little help if someone arrives at these agencies only to find their doors closed or their ability to provide services continually questionable. Moreover, rejection from helping agencies often elicits frustration and despair that cause additional problems and further street entrenchment (Forchuk et al., 2010).

Keith, for instance, revealed how consistent rejection from charitable agencies and treatment centres left him hopeless.

> I just gave up on them [service agencies] all total eh … so I sleep outside. … It is a thing about putting myself down lower to go and ask for help. When I asked for help here, when I asked the Hope Mission, when I asked from the Co-op, when I asked from the Seniors Club there, they all seemed to, you know, "Oh we haven't got nothing right now. We can't help you out right now." … I have just given up on myself, given up on putting myself, you know, open.

Keith sought countless services and addictions treatment programs. After repeatedly hearing that the agencies could not help him, he understandably grew weary. He found it emotionally difficult to "open" up, admit his problems, and seek help. When programs shut him out after he opened up to them, he felt as though he was "putting himself down lower." Even if service levels had improved, telling Keith where to go for help was of little use because consistent previous rejection from local agencies had led him to "give up" and resign himself to living outside for the indefinite future.

"Like Who Wants to Go in There?": Dangers In and Around Facilities

Homeless persons' reasons for avoiding charitable agencies stretched beyond the pain of rejection and the inability of different facilities to accommodate them. Conditions inside the charitable agencies also drove many people away. Shelters and drop-in centres are notoriously dangerous and unhealthy places (Dean & Melrose, 1999; Lyon-Callo, 2000; Mayers, 2001; Shantz, 2010). Many homeless persons do not visit support agencies because they feel unsafe in these facilities (Dean & Melrose, 1999; Mayers, 2001).

Fear of violent victimization within charitable agencies was especially palpable among participants. Most individuals said they were afraid to go to the city's main drop-in centres or shelters because of physical assaults in or near agencies. Many recounted instances where they were victimized. Jason, for example, explained:

> It is not safe … I hate going to the [inner-city shelter]. You see this mark here? [He takes off his hat to reveal a scar]. A guy cut me with a razor. I was in line, talking with a buddy of mine. We were waiting for lunch I think. … A guy comes along, tells my friend to move, elbows me … and says, "This is not a good spot, bugger off you guys." And he took our place in line. My friend turns around and because of that and out comes the razor and swish, swish [gesturing that he was cut].

This attack, alongside other victimizations he witnessed, led Jason to avoid charitable agencies altogether and sleep outside. Although remaining on the street did not remove the homeless from a high likelihood of violent victimization, the dangers surrounding many of the charitable agencies nonetheless caused them to see alleyways, parks, and sidewalks as safer places to meet their needs.

Homeless women face particularly high risks of victimization, especially for sexual assault, when they stay in shelters that serve both sexes (Goodman, Fels, Glenn, & Benitez, 2011). Kelly retold one unfortunate instance where her daughter was attacked:

> The shelters are not that good … because, well … baby girl [her daughter who is a young adult] almost got raped. [A male friend] beat the fuck out of [the rapist] because [the rapist] was trying to pull baby girl's pants down. … And now [her male friend] is banned from [the shelter] for life.

Unfortunately, homeless women sometimes stayed in mixed-sex shelters because there are insufficient numbers of women-only shelter beds (Goodman, Fels, Glenn & Benitez, 2011). The sexual assault of Kelly's daughter and the violent responses of other males demonstrate that these shelters are highly masculine and dangerous spaces. The shelters clearly do not condone such violence, as they banned the males involved for life, but the atmosphere of male violence also excludes many women from these same shelters. Kelly, for instance, did not want to risk further victimization and avoided the shelters as much as she could after the incident, preferring instead to stay outside among persons she trusted.

Other individuals avoided drops-in centres and shelters because they could not protect their personal belongings. Although homeless persons do not have much private property, many avoid support agencies because the organizations do not offer a means to secure their possessions (Dean & Melrose, 1999; Mayers, 2001). Several participants reported that their belongings were stolen from charitable agencies. Dean, for example, warned, "[G]o downtown to the shelters, I went when I first hit the streets. I was there for three days and I had everything stolen." Dan also said he avoids all the city's shelters because there is:

> too much violence, too much criminal activity. If you are not looking after your stuff, they don't have any place to lock your stuff up, so basically you are sleeping on a mat with all your stuff under it. If you leave it, it is gone. ... So anything you have with you, if you can't take it with you, you might as well just take it outside and give it to them [other facility users who are apparently thieves] because it will be gone the next day.

Although Dan's depiction of all other shelter users as thieves is problematic, he, alongside many other participants, avoided going to shelters or drop-in centers because the agencies did not appreciate that he had belongings he needed or cherished and so wanted to protect.

Other non-criminal dangers led individuals to avoid local shelters and drop-in centers. In particular, participants felt the agencies were unclean and posed health risks. According to Jeff Shantz (2010), many Canadian shelters do not meet the United Nations' guidelines for refugee camps and face epidemic levels of diseases (like Tuberculosis) that are practically eradicated in the general population. While no participants reported contracting such serious diseases from shelters, a few explained that they contracted parasites. For instance, when asked how she likes the shelters, Darlene said, "I don't. I contracted head lice from there. ... They are not very clean when I was there, that was years ago." Darlene's negative experience led her to avoid the helping agencies and live solely on the street for the next two years.

Steve also cited unclean conditions as one of the reasons he tried to avoid the local drop-in centres and shelters:

> You don't even want to go in there [a longstanding local drop-in centre] to shower. There are needles on the floor. There are blood splats on the wall. … Like who wants to go in there? That makes you feel good going in there and changing your clothes looking at a needle in the corner or a blood splat on the wall.

The sometimes unhygienic conditions of the helping agencies thus turned persons like Darlene and Keith to the street. Although sleeping rough and remaining on the streets damages health (Minaker & Hogeveen, 2009), many street-involved persons felt that staying on the streets was safer than utilizing agencies with overt markers of acute health risks like blood splats and lice outbreaks.

A few homeless persons also said they avoided the drop-in centres and shelters due to the common presence of drugs. These participants were trying to maintain healthy and sober lifestyles and did not want to deal with the temptations posed by other users and dealers who frequent the agencies. Stan, for example, explained that he avoids the charitable agencies because he does not want to be constantly pressured into selling or consuming drugs or alcohol:

> There is like, crack is everywhere, you wouldn't believe. You go to the [agency] and … people bother you. They say, "You looking for … food?" They call crack food. They say, "You looking for food?" And I say. "No." [They say,] "You looking for food? Do you know where I can find T3s? Do you know where I can find Valium? … Do you know where I can find Ativan?" Everything. "Fuck off man," [I say]. I am getting sick of it so I stay away.

The consistent pressure to consume or secure drugs is not a positive environment for those hoping to overcome addictions. Keith, who likewise tried to avoid local drop-in centres in order to manage his alcoholism, captured how attending some of the agencies can be counterproductive. He asked: "What the hell is the use of going to someplace … trying to get help, but they [facility managers] are letting them [other facility users] carry on their substance abuse?" Agencies that operate on harm reduction philosophies and serve persons with ongoing addictions often make significant improvements in the lives of some marginalized persons (Darlene James Policy & Business Planning, 2007; Evans, 2012), yet the city also needs agencies that align with the perspectives of people like Stan and Keith who feel they need to distance themselves from drugs.

That some participants had been victimized, had contracted parasites, had encountered visible symbols of health risks, or had been pressured into drug use inside the services, demonstrates the dangers among these agencies. These dangers highlight the gravity of the rhetorical question Steve asks above when describing "blood splats" on the wall of a local drop-in centre: "Like who wants to go in there?" In truth, very few people want to go to these facilities. Homeless persons should not be expected to endure conditions that most persons would rather avoid. When the homeless avoid these agencies they act in the same manner that many housed persons would act. They are avoiding the agencies in order to protect themselves.

"I Was Happier on the Street": Services Out of Sync with Many Homeless Persons' Lives

Participants' who did accept the risks within charitable agencies and accessed services revealed that the manner in which services were delivered also led some homeless persons to prefer participation in the informal economy. In particular, many of the rules and policies of programs upset homeless persons. Social services and housing programs police the homeless through a gamut of rules and contractual-like programs aimed at behavioural reform (Hermer, 2001; Lyon-Callo, 2000; Whiteford, 2010). In fact, some homeless-serving agencies make access to material aid contingent upon following particular institutional policies (Whiteford, 2010).

Homeless Edmontonians confirmed that behavioural rules guarded access to most services. They revealed a long list of rules that they had to uphold to utilize drop-in centres, shelters, housing programs, and addictions services. Some of these rules, such as mandatory sign-ins or prohibitions on parties, resembled standard rental/use agreements. Other rules, however, excessively restricted and interfered with homeless persons' everyday lives.

For example, housing workers evicted Jason from his room in a long-term men's shelter because he used the payphone too often. He explained:

So I went down there [to the housing agency], applied, it was a great place. But the guy that runs the program from there turned out to be a real jerk. They got three phones in the place. There is one that is free for the residents to use. There are two others and they are paid for. Those two phones are rarely used because you can use the free ones. But I avoided that one … because I hate waiting in line for that thing because I can't remember anything. [He suffers from short-term memory loss due to previous alcoholism]. For me it is rush, rush, rush. So I go and use one of the payphones, and the guy that runs the programs says … "What are you doing? … Don't do that anymore." … The next day, or the day after, whenever, I forgot all about what he said. The next day I am phoning some government agency. He comes up behind me and he … slams the receiver down. I said, "What the hell did you do that for?" He says, "You are evicted, get out of here. … I warned you not to use the pay phone."

Jason was attending to important personal business. He required the payphone to function with his short-term memory loss. Program administrators, however, did not appreciate this and evicted him for disobeying their requests that he stop. The behavioural guidelines workers imposed did not coincide with Jason's needs and so he was unable to act in the fashion they demanded. The agency's rules cast him into absolute homelessness.

The helping agencies also dictate the daily routines of the street-involved by setting specific hours of operation. Shelters commonly force residents to leave during breakfast hours, while drop-in centres are typically only open during standard daytime business hours. These early wake-up calls and limited hours are constant complaints among shelter users (Dean & Melrose, 1999; Mayers, 2001). For many homeless persons the different agencies' hours create a repetitive daily cycle among the helping institutions (DeVerteuil, 2003). Some participants disliked this monotony and so tried to avoid the shelters and drop-in centres. They preferred to determine the structure of their day, including when it started. Mike conveyed this position when he proclaimed, "I prefer to stay outside … because I can sleep in. I don't have to wake up at a certain time to get kicked out. I could sleep all day if I want." Although police and passersby awoke persons who slept outside just as early shelters did, Mike and others nonetheless felt that they held more control over daily routines than they would if they utilized shelters. The rules of the shelter did not meet their preferences and did not allow them to feel like autonomous adults.

Forced programming within agencies also undercuts homeless adults' autonomy. Most of the city's housing programming draws on a Housing First philosophy which proclaims that addictions counselling and other services should not be preconditions for shelter (Evans, 2012; Homeward Trust Edmonton, 2012; Klodawsky, 2009). Nonetheless, a few participants reported that self-help programming was still a requirement of local housing programs. Darlene, for instance, explained that workers from her housing program hold keys to her apartment and twice barged into her place to tell her that she had to seek addictions treatment.

> Well one time, twice, they [her housing caseworkers] walked in on me in the middle of the night, while I was sleeping, when there were no problems. … And they said, "You are not looking too well. You got to go to detox for three days." And like I really got upset with them. I told them, "Ok I will go, but I was happier on the street than I am here."

Darlene shows how forced programming can be counterproductive and so ought not to be a requirement of shelter. The workers want Darlene to lead a healthy lifestyle. Their efforts to push her into this lifestyle, however, jeopardize her sense of autonomy. As such, she becomes frustrated and unhappy, declaring that she "was happier on the street" where Housing First staff did not tell her what do.

Ensuring homeless persons complete programming and abide by agency rules requires heavy surveillance regimes that can undermine clients' sense of privacy (Lyon-Callo, 2000). Obtrusive oversight was particularly apparent among street-involved individuals who secured housing through charitable agencies. Steve, for example, described how, like Darlene, housing caseworkers were constantly watching over him:

> I have never gotten a piece of mail that they haven't opened. They held back a cheque for two weeks, even my fucking cable bill they are opening. Like it really pisses me off. … I never asked you to open that. … It's like I don't know what these peoples' problems are, but they are invading all my privacy, they are invading all my rights … they are not allowed to do that.

He later added:

> I go for a walk and come back and they [program workers] are telling me about it three days later. "We counted you going in and out 17 times in three days," [they said to me]. I said, "Who gives a fuck? You know, I am allowed to come and go as I want."

Steve bemoaned that he "didn't sign up for this" and that caseworkers patronize him. He declared, "They try to manipulate your life and try to control it."

The surveillance and control in many programs was so severe that some participants, like Keith and Darlene, described their encounters with the helping agencies through the language of criminal justice. Darlene, for example, described her involvement with the housing program as being on "probation." While the caseworkers might indeed call the early period of her housing program probationary, this term demonstrates the continued police function and loss of autonomy that accompanies much of the programming aimed at the street-involved (Feldman, 2004). A loss of autonomy and privacy irritated the homeless who used social services and led many to question if they would remain in housing programming.

Several individuals found attending drop-in centers or soup kitchens humiliating and felt that these places also stripped them of their autonomy. Nick, for example, said:

> I just don't like the idea of it. One time too, uh, I went to one [agency] over here [north of downtown] … they had you line up for breakfast. I said, "Fuck this I am not in the army." You had to sign up for lunch and all that. No, bye.

Nick's declaration that he is "not in the army" shows that he views the procedures surrounding free meals as analogous to those of the military barracks. Signing up to get into the agency and then lining up for lunch stripped him of his sense of individuality and freedom much like the experiences cadets undergo as they are resocialized during basic training (Ashforth, Sluss & Harrison, 2007, p. 8). Nick left because he did not like the embarrassing feeling the agency cast upon him. Steve further explained this feeling:

> You know I don't like going to these soup kitchens and that. I feel degraded half the time. We just went to the [shelter] last Monday for breakfast and I hadn't been in there in over a year and I felt humiliated and that just being there.

The loss of autonomy and stigma accompanying the use of support agencies leaves Steve feeling depressed and humiliated. Like Nick and many others, Steve preferred to avoid the charitable agencies and meet his needs through the informal economy.

Informal Economy and Autonomous Consumption Preferred

Given the patronizing rules, rigid hours, forced programming, and heavy surveillance within helping agencies, it is perhaps unsurprising that many homeless persons feel stigmatized by social service use (Lyon-Callo, 2000) and prefer to engage in informal economic activity. For instance, panhandling often gave the homeless more personal satisfaction than using services. Participants preferred to purchase shelter or goods with the money they received in the informal economy over sleeping on mats or waiting in lines at organizations for food and services they could not choose. Like most people, homeless persons want to have a say in their consumption

(Gaetz, Tarasuk, Dachner & Kirkpatrick, 2006, p. 52). In particular, many individuals wanted to determine what they ate or what they did with their money. Vaughn, for example told me, that he panhandled "for food and coffee" because he "would rather eat out" so that he could choose his food and eat alone with "no line up."

Consumption is an important means through which many people construct and evaluate identities (Feldman, 2004; Hayward, 2004; Hayward & Yar, 2006; Rose, 1990). Homeless persons felt embarrassed when they could not freely participate in consumption and had to rely on social services or strangers to secure consumer goods. Marie, for instance, avoided the charitable agencies in part because she wanted to be a consumer. She further explained that she felt embarrassed when strangers bought her the things she needed.

> I prefer money because sometimes I get embarrassed going in and like, you know what I mean, shopping like that with somebody I don't know. But if worse comes to worse I am not going to turn it down either. ... Yeah, if I am really hungry, like I feel better to buy it on my own, but if I am really hungry I will go in and just ... pick out something quick.

Marie's preference to panhandle in order to "buy it on her own" reveals how homeless persons are simultaneously included and excluded from consumer society. She felt the pressure to be a consumer, but her poverty excluded her from easily purchasing consumer goods on her own. She sought cash in hand through panhandling (an activity that marked her exclusion) so that she could purchase goods on her own and exercise a consumer subjectivity (an activity that made her feel included and "better").

Efforts to integrate homeless persons like Marie into the helping agencies thus overlook how the street-involved experience the social service sector and the informal economy. For some, the informal economy more immediately allows them to partake in individual consumption, which offers a greater sense of happiness, autonomy, and respect. Trying to push homeless persons into charities denies their desires to be their own consumers.

Programs Ignored Homeless Persons' Social Lives

Homeless individuals hopes of being autonomous should not, however, reinforce assumptions that they are simply atomistic and unattached individuals. It is a common stereotype to view the homeless as solitary, transient drifters who do not establish meaningful personal connections (Cresswell, 2011). The programming, rules, and surveillance of homeless-serving organizations often take these ostensibly asocial individual as their focus (Lyon-Callo, 2000; Whiteford, 2010). Homeless persons, however, do not exist as disconnected individuals but instead establish many important social bonds (Duneier, 2001; Lankenau, 1999b; Mayers, 2001; Tanner, 2009) that agencies ought to acknowledge.

Social ties ran deep among participants. All but two individuals reported having a network of friends – a "street family" (Tanner, 2009) – that they consistently hung out with. These groups often offer protection and share resources (Tanner, 2009). In fact, although the streets are dangerous, a culture of sharing also surrounds homeless persons. During several interviews I witnessed homeless persons sharing the limited food, drink, and money they had with other street-involved persons. For example, while I interviewed Nick he gave money from his panhandling collection to a friend so that the friend could secure food and cigarettes for himself. He tells me:

> I met [friend] down here. I met him this year. He goes and gets my pop if I need it or coffee. ... We work our little deal. ... I help out those that I know need. ... And that is the kinda thing that goes on down here. They will pay back another day. One day he will do something for me, you know. And if everybody did that, it would be great.

Carl confirmed that street people often help each other out. As I interviewed him, Steve, whom I interviewed at an earlier point, approached to see how I was doing. The two did not know one another. As soon as they were introduced, Carl immediately began to share the food I had just given him with Steve. Carl explained how this gesture was common among the street-involved. He said, "I get a lot of compassion from people, street people.... Yeah, we watch out for each other." Looking after one another helps the homeless ensure survival (Tanner, 2009).

Unfortunately most local programming did not appreciate that homeless persons held meaningful social ties. For instance, one of the most common rules that housed but street-involved persons struggled with was a "no visitors" policy. Darlene's housing program, for example, does not let Keith, her long-time partner who has no housing, stay at her place. Keith admitted that they can have an "argumentative lifestyle" but explained that instead of working with the couple, housing caseworkers "figure we should not be together and are doing everything in their damnest to keep us apart." In one instance caseworkers "invaded [Darlene's] home at 3 o'clock or 3:30 in the morning" because they "heard he was there." Darlene explained how important being with others is to her. She said, "I don't really care for the rules because I come from a large family. I am always with people. Living alone, what is the sense?" She explained that she feels lonely in the unit where she cannot have guests and so she comes out to the street daily to visit Keith and other acquaintances.

Another participant, Steve, faced eviction and absolute homelessness for having an unapproved guest stay in his housing unit.

> I have been doing good and it feels good to have a place but these people [housing caseworkers] are driving me back outside … because they don't like my girlfriend. … They said, "We bumped her to the top of the list [for the same housing programming] and she missed that appointment, so now we banned her from the building." … Banned! … Literally they threw her out the door and said, "I'll phone the cops if she comes back here." … I want her off the street. … Already they tried to evict me twice because I snuck her in twice. … They gave me an eviction notice for the 7th. … I don't know what is going to happen, like am I going to be homeless again? … I am totally stressed about it.

Like most participants, Steve held important relationships with other persons, particularly other homeless persons. Many of these people, especially Marie, he dearly cared for.

Program workers often failed to grasp the significance of the social bonds clients held with other homeless persons. Steve, for instance, described his love for Marie and his frustration over caseworkers' inability to accept this caring relationship:

> You know, I get her phoning me crying and I can't let her in. And I do let her in. I tell these guys [housing caseworkers] that and they go, "Well you should be stronger than that. No is no. … You should worry about yourself more than your girlfriend." I said, "Why don't you worry about yourself instead of your wife?" … Somebody phones you and tells you that your girlfriend is lying in a park, and she is freezing cold, and she is soaking wet. … I went downtown and got her, threw her in a cab and brought her back to my place after she was banned. [The caseworker] goes, "Well I would have left her there." I said, "Well you would have left her there but I wouldn't. That is somebody I love and care about.… I will do that a thousand times over again." He said, "Good, that is why we are evicting you." … [I said,] "I don't care. You don't love her, but I do. And if I got to be homeless with her, well fine." … Like last week I spent four days on the street with her, sleeping in parks and stuff like that, because she's not allowed at my place. And because I want to be with her we got to sleep outside. Meanwhile, I got a place. It doesn't make sense. I pay rent for it. It's frustrating.

Steve has been living on the streets for the past four days because he cannot take the person he loved to his unit in the subsidized housing program. He feels a great duty to help this person and wants to care for her, so he snuck her into his shelter and consequently received an eviction notice. That the housing workers do not understand how important this relationship is to Steve is clear when they suggest that he should leave her to freeze in a park. The caseworkers demonstrated that they viewed Steve as ideally unattached when they told him to be "stronger" and "worry about himself more."

Persons like Steve, however, are not disconnected from others and their ties to street families did not end when they secured housing. Instead, formerly-homeless persons found that affluence and access to shelter strengthened their desire to help other homeless persons. Steve explained how the culture of care among street families compelled many persons to share their shelter with others:

> That whole building that I live in, everybody and their brothers' got the same program. Buddy is homeless and they got two bedrooms in there. They won't house two of them together, they house one each. But he gets in shit for letting his buddy sleep on the couch. Meanwhile, buddy and his friend had been homeless for five years together. Anytime buddy got money and could put him in a motel, he did – back and forth like that. So how are you just going to forget about your friend and leave him stand out in the rain or cold?

Steve describes the "back and forth" reciprocal ties that comprise many street relationships. These ties led many formerly-homeless but now-housed persons to break "no visitors" policies in order to extend shelter to persons who helped them while they were homeless. If they could not offer shelter to their still-homeless associates, they often felt as though they were abandoning friends who helped them when they were in need.

Housing caseworkers' narrow focus on individual clients like Steve or Darlene failed to realize that a full understanding of homeless persons includes their relationships with others. Denying these social bonds meant that several housed participants remained tied to the streets so that they could be among their long-time friends and partners. Rules and assumptions among agencies that reinforce images of homeless persons as solitary hobos thus pushed them away from charities and onto streets where they could maintain the relationships they cared about.

Conclusion: Recommendations to Align Services with Homeless Persons' Lives

The stories and lived experiences of participants reveal that persuading people to direct the homeless to the charitable agencies is not as straightforward and helpful as broken windows theorists and other anti-panhandling supporters like the EPS and HHGS campaign officials suggest. If and when the homeless approached the helping agencies, they often encountered closed doors, inappropriately aligned services, victimization, and acute health risks that turned them back to the street. Inside agencies individuals frequently found themselves policed through patronizing rules and forced programming. Given the stigma surrounding social service use, some homeless persons saw involvement in the informal economy as a less humiliating way to achieve a consumer subjectivity that held more autonomy than clients of social services. Additionally, many participants lived social lives and refused to fully integrate into services so they could continue to care for members of their street families. Messages that proclaim that homeless persons ought to simply avail themselves of local charities overlook all these service shortages, gaps, and shortcomings.

Without recognizing the factors that hinder service use, visible homelessness is constructed as a voluntary condition that individuals simply need to be coerced out of through bylaw enforcement and the cessation of direct monetary aid (Feldman, 2004). When it is acknowledged that various service barriers turn individuals back to the street, their presence in public spaces cannot be as easily depicted as a lifestyle choice. All participants demonstrated how the limited capacity of charitable agencies, service gaps, lingering dangers, and misguided rules contributed to their remaining homeless. Darlene, however, best illuminated how these conditions complicated any depiction of her visible homelessness as voluntary. When asked what the most important message she wanted to convey to housed persons about homelessness was, she quickly replied, "I am a survivor. ... I used to eat out of the garbage. ... You are not always given a choice, you have to survive." Her parting words, coupled with the multiple barriers homeless persons face in accessing essential needs such as food, are stark reminders that her presence and actions on the streets are not simply her decisions but instead reflect several policy and programming failures that must be addressed.

Of course, this study's participants reflect those individuals least likely to integrate into social services and so were unlikely to present the successes of local charitable organizations. To be fair, a few local charitable organizations might do better jobs at welcoming the homeless (see, for e.g., Hogeveen & Freistadt, 2013). Nonetheless, the stories of these relatively more street entrenched persons expose several shortcomings in service provision and, more importantly, reveal possible ways to improve social services.

In particular, the experiences of the homeless suggest that increased government funding to the poor and to social services would be extremely beneficial. Increased income assistance to the homeless would allow them to avoid charitable agencies altogether and to express the autonomous consumer subjectivity they desire. Participants worked in the informal economy in order to receive cash that they could use as they saw fit. Adequate direct financial aid from the government would be more reliable than monetary donations from passersby and would allow more complete participation in the acts of consumption that are central to many individuals' sense of worth.

The social service agencies also need a considerable injection of resources. Guaranteed long-term funding that keeps administration of programs in stable and predictable places would remove some of the dizzying chaos homeless persons experienced as they cycled in and out of housing programs that were continually changing hands. Overall the level of services – of drop-in centres, soup kitchens, emergency shelter beds, addictions treatment spaces, and independent housing programming – needs to increase. There is a particularly sharp need for more women-only shelters and programs. The city's marginalized also need adequate options for both "wet" programs, which attend to intoxicated persons, and "dry" programs, which prohibit drug and alcohol consumption.

Homeless-serving agencies should also improve their ability to provide safe facilities that remain welcoming environments. Agencies face the difficult task of simultaneously reducing the surveillance, crime, and health risks within their facilities if they wish to remain spaces that appeal to all homeless persons. To this end, shelters and drop-in centres could reduce theft by developing a means to store and protect clients' belongings (Duneier, 2001). Additionally, if services better integrated homeless persons into their program design and delivery, clients would likely feel more welcomed and would better retain the sense of adult autonomy they desire. The homeless might also feel as though they remain autonomous adults, and not patronized clients, if the rules surrounding programs were more flexible. Forcing individuals to undergo programming is particularly disastrous to their sense of autonomy. For that reason Homeward Trust Edmonton, which funds the city's housing programs, needs to set in place mechanisms that ensure programs truly follow the Housing First philosophy which rejects programming as a condition for accessing shelter. Finally, agencies would align more with the lived realities of the homeless if they offered 24/7 services and did not limit their hours in order to structure their clients' days.

Charitable agencies, especially those that provide housing, need to appreciate the social bonds that surround homelessness. Homeless persons are not solitary hobos and often desire to care for others. Programs for the homeless ought to focus less on individuals and instead work with the groups and relationships that comprise homeless persons' lives. Couples and group programming exists for housed families, but is apparently lacking for homeless persons. Participant's stories demonstrate that their lives unfold in relationships with others. Agencies must care for all these other persons if they wish to adequately care for any single person. In this sense, it is imperative that programs find safe housing arrangements for the social ties of any one homeless person. Moreover, housing provision requires more diverse shelter options (Feldman, 2004). The focus on individual apartments that dominates current housing policy overlooks the fact that some homeless persons might prefer more communal living arrangements (Klodawsky, 2009).

Without attending to the shortcomings among social services, efforts to encourage individuals to divert homeless persons to local charities will continue to fall short. Broken windows theorists, EPS agents, and HHGS campaign officials make problematic assumptions about street life when they proclaim that current services are sufficient to resolve homelessness. In fact, their failure to even acknowledge the current problems among charities contradicts their alleged intent to ensure "real" help for the homeless (City of Edmonton, 2010b). Rather, the blind faith anti-panhandling supporters appear to have in charitable organizations suggests these actors hope to push the homeless into agencies and out of sight (Mayers, 2001) or aim to depicted the homeless as persons who must be coerced into helping themselves (Feldman, 2004).

CHAPTER FOUR

"IF YOU ARE HOMELESS, OF COURSE YOU STAND OUT MORE IN THE CROWD": LOOKING OUT OF PLACE IN CONSUMER SPACES DREW POLICE ATTENTION REGARDLESS OF ACTIONS OR RELATIONS TO WAGE LABOUR

The stories of Edmonton's homeless challenge the claims of broken windows theorists and others who support anti-homeless measures, yet those who defend anti-panhandling laws such as Edmonton's revised Public Places Bylaw (2009) would contend that these laws are legitimate because they do not target the homeless persons I interviewed but instead focus on a subset of aggressive panhandlers. The EPS, for instance, repeatedly declared that "the amendment to the Public Places Bylaw would deal specifically with aggressive panhandling" and that non-aggressive homeless persons "would not be impacted" (Elanik, 2009, p. 2, 3). City lawyer Steve Phipps also proclaimed that Edmonton's new anti-panhandling bylaw was valid because unlike earlier vagrancy laws it focused on "belligerent behaviour, rather than banning all begging" (Kent, 2009, p. A1). Such claims assert that because anti-panhandling laws are behaviour-based they are not anti-homeless ordinances but simply means of maintaining order by reducing aggressive actions.

Scholars behind the production of the proletariat argument and the civic sanitation argument, however, contend that new anti-panhandling ordinances, despite their focus on behaviour, single out homeless persons. According to Todd Gordon's (2006, p. 38, 67) production of the proletariat argument, anti-panhandling laws are resurrected, albeit reworded, vagrancy statutes that criminalize the "able-bodied and unemployed" who reject work ethic and refuse to "endure the discipline of the wage." For Gordon, it is not the behaviour of panhandlers and homeless persons that draws police attention, but what they don't do: engage in wage labour. As such, anti-panhandling laws, like early vagrancy laws, apparently aim to push the street-involved into the "worst paying and most dead-end, unsatisfying, and insecure forms of market work" (Gordon, 2010, p. 38).

The civic sanitation argument set out by authors like Don Mitchell (1997, 2004), Mario Berti and Jeff Sommers (2010), Damian Collins and Nicholas Blomley (2003), Leonard Feldman (2004), Janet Mosher (2002), and William O'Grady, Stephen Gaetz, and Kristy Buccieri (2011), in contrast, concedes that many anti-panhandling laws, alongside other anti-homeless ordinances, focus on behaviours. This position observes, however, that the behaviours that these laws are concerned with – such as asking for money, sleeping, and defecating – are necessary for survival and are only outlawed when completed in public spaces. Since homeless persons live most of their days in public spaces and must eventually engage in these actions, they are the primary targets of these laws (Mitchell, 1997, 2004). As such, these laws, despite their behaviour-based language, are anti-homeless ordinances that try to remove homeless persons from public space. Moreover, according to the civic sanitation argument, efforts to expel the homeless from public space occur in order to appease business leaders who hope the cleansing of public space will attract more consumers and investment (Berti & Sommers, 2010; Collins & Blomley, 2003; Mitchell, 2004). As O'Grady, Gaetz and Buccieri (2011, p. 13) explain, anti-panhandling laws mean that "people who are deemed by police officers to be homeless, because of how they look, what they are doing, and where they are doing it ... [are] singled out for greater scrutiny or differential treatment."

This chapter helps untangle these different views on anti-panhandling laws by examining how homeless persons come in contact with police officers. It uses the stories of the homeless to document whether policing, as it unfolds on the street, aims at aggressive and threatening behaviour, at persons who refuse wage labour, or at visibly homeless persons who occupy prime spaces. Do Edmonton police limit their use of the revised Public Places Bylaw (2009) to aggressive panhandlers as they contend? Or do officers single out homeless persons regardless of behaviour? Are the homeless who encounter police unemployed? Do their relations to wage labour affect how police officers respond to them? Does being or looking homeless while in consumer spaces result in police attention? Are there other reasons consumers spaces are central to the policing of homelessness beside the fact that they are the areas in which powerful business agents demand the police remove the homeless?

I address these questions and argue that Edmonton's anti-panhandling law enables police officers to target homeless persons based not on their behaviour, nor their relations to wage labour, but their appearance as out of place in prime consumer spaces. This argument proceeds through three steps. First, I detail how homeless persons drew the attention of police officers. This section reveals that, despite arguments that anti-panhandling laws deal with aggressive behaviour, these laws target homeless persons. Second, I contend that police attention had more to do with visible homelessness in consumer spaces than with homeless person's relations to wage labour. The current policing of homelessness does not verify if individuals are capable of working and refuse to do so, nor does it force upon the homeless a previously-absent work ethic. Rather, simply looking homeless in consumer space garnered police attention – whether able-bodied or not and regardless of employment status. This discussion challenges the production of the proletariat argument and aligns more closely with the civic sanitation argument. However, I discuss how some homeless persons who upheld the appearance of consumers avoided police contact and in so doing I build on the civic sanitation argument by showing that the policing of homelessness requires consumer spaces to provide a backdrop against which homeless-looking persons stand out. Finally, I conclude by echoing the civic sanitation argument's call to create inclusive spaces but I also contend that doing so must attend to several shortcomings that the remaining chapters address.

Police Did Not Target Aggressive Panhandlers

Participants' stories challenge claims that police use anti-panhandling laws to only target aggressive panhandlers. Police often stopped, questioned, ticketed, or informally sanctioned panhandlers regardless of how they were panhandling. Nick, for instance, sits against a building with a cup out on the sidewalk. There is plenty of room to get around him. He doesn't ask for money and typically only speaks if someone else initiates conversation. In some cases his actions are so subtle that people do not understand that he is panhandling. He explained, for example, that when passersby see his collection cup in front of him on the sidewalk, many ask, "What is that for?" They are hardly aware that he is panhandling and so would struggle to label his actions as aggressive panhandling. Nonetheless, Nick reported, "I had a cop question me the other day, a couple weeks ago. This is the first time I have been bothered in 5 years." The officer eventually told Nick that he had to pack up and leave. The police harassed Nick because they understood him to be panhandling, not because of the way he was panhandling. Nick was not acting aggressively, yet the officer apparently felt he should now dissuade all panhandlers.

In some cases panhandlers received fines for passively panhandling. Joseph described one instance where police officers ticketed him simply for asking someone for money:

> On Whyte Ave dude, the cops … some of them I get along with. But there are the fucking assholes that are like … "What were you just asking that person? Were you asking them for money?" And I was, but I was like, "Um, no." … And [they said], "Well, we are going to write you a ticket."

Joseph's actions did not contravene the anti-panhandling provisions of Edmonton's Public Places Bylaw (2009). The police saw Joseph ask another person for money but they did not witness an aggressive request. Nonetheless, police officers issued him a $250 anti-aggressive-panhandling ticket. Joseph bemoaned, "Like I can understand" receiving a ticket "if I am harassing people hardcore." He did not feel, however, that this instance justified a fine. When I told Joseph the bylaw's intent is to sanction only aggressive persons, he simply conceded "but that is what they do … with me."

Police officers told many participants that they could not request money regardless of the manner in which they asked. Russ, for instance, said that he got a ticket for panhandling simply because he was asking a person for money. He explained, "I didn't really realize … a police officer was right there. He [the officer] said. 'Right now buddy you are asking for change.' And … because I was doing that he wrote me up a ticket." Steve similarly explained that officers warned him and his girlfriend Marie, "Listen if you ask for money we can give you a ticket."

Joseph and Russ received fines, and Marie and Steve got warnings, because they relied on panhandling. The manner in which they sought aid was irrelevant. Simply asking for money was enough to receive a ticket or draw additional police attention.

Anti-panhandling laws often set out broad definitions of aggressive requests that grant considerable police discretion (Hermer & Mosher, 2002). This discretion potentially explains some of these cases where officers sanction seemingly passive solicitations. Officers might have felt the requests were indeed aggressive. In many cases, however, panhandlers did not have to be actively requesting money to draw police attention.

Rick, for instance, recalled one instance where he was not asking for money but officers accused him of panhandling and fined him nonetheless:

> You know what they are cracking down on me for? Panhandling. ... I actually got a ticket for panhandling ... $250 fine or something like that. ... Two weeks ago. They [police officers] seen me sitting outside [restaurant]. They said, "What are you doing? We think you are panhandling." ... I was just sitting there. I wasn't even panhandling actually when they come, they seen me sitting there hey. But they seen me there day after day, you know?

Rick was just sitting in public space when officers fined him. He was not requesting money in an aggressive manner. This is particularly clear when the officers said to Rick, "We think you are panhandling." The police officers were themselves unsure if Rick was currently panhandling. If it was not clear that he was panhandling, then how could the officers determine that he was aggressively panhandling? Nevertheless, police used the bylaw and Rick's known status as a panhandler to issue him a $250 fine.

Stories such as these reveal how, despite the fact that Edmonton's revised Public Places Bylaw (2009) focuses on aggressive panhandling, police officers used the bylaw to dissuade and punish all panhandling. It was not, as EPS authorities claimed, only "belligerent beggars" (Inspector Nowlan in Hanon, 2009, n.p.) that received fines, but many passive panhandlers too. Rick confirmed that he felt police used the bylaw to target all panhandlers. He said police are "cracking down ... on all panhandlers as far as I know."

The stories of other participants, however, suggest that Rick's declaration that all panhandlers face police action is still too narrow. In several instances, homeless persons who never or very seldom panhandled were accused of panhandling and subject to police attention. Dean, who predominately spent his days picking bottles, described one such encounter:

> One day I was, well I was bottle picking by [coffee shop] and like I wasn't panning at all. I was just in the alley and about a block down from [coffee shop] and the police pull up. And [the officers said,] "Oh, you were panhandling at [coffee shop]". I said, "No, I wasn't." And he said, "Well we got a report that you were panhandling." And this woman that had seen me picking bottles, she come out, and she said, "No, he has been picking bottles. I know him, he doesn't panhandle."

The woman's intervention prevented police from further sanctioning Dean. Nonetheless he was often stopped, accused of panhandling, and questioned. He told me that officers have accused him of panhandling and stopped him for questioning "three or four times." Police commonly stop persons who look homeless for questioning and to run them through the system (Beckett & Herbert, 2009; O'Grady, Gaetz & Buccieri, 2011).

Dean's story reveals that the anti-panhandling bylaw provides police officers another means to "stop and search" the homeless.

Participants' encounters with officers thus testify that Edmonton's anti-aggressive-panhandling bylaw is used to target homeless persons. Joe Hermer and Janet Mosher (2002) speculate that the broad definitions of solicitation and aggressive behaviour in most anti-panhandling laws mean that some persons who simply look needy could be seen as requesting aid and so accused of aggressive panhandling. Homeless persons who did not panhandle, or were not currently panhandling, but were still accused of doing so corroborate this position. As Dean succinctly explained, a lot of police officers "think that just because you are homeless you are automatically a panhandler." Officers used concerns over panhandling to justify ticketing, threatening, and moving the homeless.

Policing Visible Homelessness in Consumer Spaces, Not Employment Status

Gordon (2006, 2010) contends that being homeless draws police attention because it overlaps with the police force's historical objective of enforcing wage labour. For Gordon it is not the visible poverty of homelessness that concerns police, but the fact that homeless persons reject wage labour when they could be working in low-skilled jobs. Participant's stories, however, also challenged this position.

In particular, the experiences of the homeless do not align with Gordon's suggestion that homelessness excludes work ethic or paid employment. The homeless often hold conventional views about employment (Gaetz & O'Grady, 2002). Most participants wanted to secure meaningful jobs. Debrah, for instance, declared that she would "prefer to get a home and get a job" above all else. Staci likewise dreamed of "going ... back to work." She proclaimed, "I want to go back doing my marketing," a profession she held decades before she became homeless.

Additionally, many homeless persons feel that their involvement in the informal economy is akin to wage labour and requires a hard work ethic (Chard, Faulkner & Chugg, 2009; Duneier, 2001; Gaetz & O'Grady, 2002; Gowan, 2009). Keith, for instance, viewed vending the streets news as work and defended it as such. He said:

> I often tell [Darlene], I am doing a good job, everybody tells me. She says, "Ah that is not working." To me it is. You stand out there for 8 hours a day in the sun; that takes a lot off you.

Similarly, Tina declared that panhandling was like work and, like any work, involved rules and routines. When asked why she preferred to panhandle over other options, she said, "Maybe it is some of the rules I make. It is like a job and I follow my rules."

The repetitive daily schedules of informal economic activity resemble the spatially and temporally organized routines of many unskilled labourers (Duneier, 2001; Gowan, 2009). Homeless persons who participate in the informal economy have places to be, times they have to be there, and conventions that they follow. Keith sold the papers "8 hours a day" and Tina's "job" as a panhandler was bound by the same rules every day. Homeless persons thus did not "consciously try to avoid the drudgery of wage work" as Gordon (2010, p. 38) suggests. Rather, they aspired to, or were already inscribed in, similar daily practices.

Moreover, some persons who participate in the informal economy also engage in paid employment (Gaetz & O'Grady, 2002). Several participants, for instance, relied on casual employment or day labour programs as part of their income-generating activities. Bob, for example, worked causally as a bricklayer and panhandled to supplement his income because the few companies he worked for did not "have enough work this year." Stan similarly struggled to survive through precarious low-skilled labour. He explained, "I go to Labour Ready ... because I only got grade 6." Nevertheless, he occasionally panhandled because he only received inconsistent and poorly-paid work through the job-placement agency.

Gordon's (2006, 2010) contention that anti-panhandling laws seek to punish those who subsist outside of ties to wage labour thus problematically assumes that individuals could live strictly off income generated in wage labour or in the informal economy. Many homeless persons, however, patched together several income-generating activities to make ends meet, including the precarious wage labour that Gordon argues anti-homeless laws seek to encourage. While Gordon understands the precariousness of the new economy, he overlooks the fact that this precariousness often necessitates participation in banned activities. Outlawing participation in the informal economy does not simply push homeless people into wage labour (Gaetz & O'Grady, 2002). Precarious wage labour and informal economic activities are connected in ways that Gordon's position glosses over.

Even those homeless persons who were fully integrated into wage labour and completely separated themselves from the informal economy were not immune from police sanction. There is a growing contingent of employed homeless persons (Shier, Jones & Graham, 2012) and these persons continued to draw police attention because of their visible poverty in prime spaces. Darlene's story, for example, demonstrated that involvement in wage labour did not protect her from police agents:

> Well, one time, [Keith] and I, we weren't panhandling at the time. I had gone to work and we were sitting on the street bench off Whyte Avenue. We ordered up [a] slice of pizza each. And the police van drove, comes storming right in, started accusing us of panhandling and drinking. And I said that wasn't what was going on. They threw [Keith] in the van, handcuffed him, threw him in, and they said, "Come on, you too." That was me. I got in and helped [Keith].

The police use panhandling as a cover to pick up Darlene and Keith, neither of whom were panhandling. Keith refused to panhandle and instead vended the street newspaper, while Darlene used to panhandle but was not panhandling at the time because she had found some clerical work through a temporary job placement agency. Police officers, however, accused Darlene and Keith of panhandling and confined them to a police van without considering their relationships to employment.

Just as police did not verify the employment status of the homeless, neither did they discern homeless persons' ability to partake in wage labour. This muddies Gordon's (2006, p. 38) suggestion that anti-homeless ordinances target the "able-bodied" in an effort to punish those who could work but refuse wage labour. In fact, all individuals whose looked homeless received police attention whether or not they were able-bodied or capable of working. Nick, for example, relied on a wheelchair to get around and so would have great difficulty in the low-skilled precarious labour Gordon (2006, 2010) says anti-panhandling laws promote. Nonetheless, once the Public Places Bylaw (2009) came into force police stopped him and told him to leave the area. Carl, Dean, Dan, and Keith, alongside most other participants, also suffered from debilitating health conditions that curtailed their ability to secure consistent employment, yet they found themselves navigating anti-homeless ordinances and other police action. Participants' ability to work menial wage labour did not distinguish who drew police attention.

The stories of the homeless suggest that Gordon's efforts to tie policing to its historical function of commodifying wage labour overlook important historical differences between vagrancy laws and current anti-panhandling laws. Unlike early vagrancy laws, existing bylaw enforcement does not contain mechanisms to confirm individuals' relationships to the means of production (Feldman, 2004). It operates on the basis of who looks homeless. Current bylaws do not criminalize being unemployed and instead instigate fines or informal police actions without examining employment status. In contrast, vagrancy laws criminalized idleness, made exceptions for the disabled, and allowed judges to use the court process to determine if individuals were working (Feldman, 2004). If accused persons were able-bodied and working or actively looking for work, judges often released them or subjected them to less punishment (Bright, 1995; Foote, 1956).

The Policing of Homelessness Requires Contrast

What the policing of homeless appears to be targeting in these cases is not individuals' relations to wage labour as the production of the proletariat argument asserts, but their appearance as homeless in prime space as the civic sanitation argument contends. Darlene most explicitly articulated this connection between her appearance and the reactions of police officers. After telling me the above story where officers removed her and Keith from Whyte Avenue in a police van, she explained her homeless appearance in that space subjected her, Keith, and other homeless persons to additional police attention. When asked why she felt the police approached her in this instance despite the fact she was not breaking any laws, she sadly explained, "Well being more dirty … or if you are homeless, of course you stand out more in the crowd." It was her visible homelessness which made her "stand out" that got her quickly expelled from the prime space of Old Strathcona.

Police agents often assume that homeless persons are unkempt, dirty, wear worn clothing, and have poor hygiene (O'Grady, Gaetz & Buccieri, 2011). Feldman (2004) observes that these appearances contrast with consumer spaces where conspicuous consumption is often glorified and consumers frequently seek to secure the latest fashionable clothing. Indeed, police contact with homeless persons apparently hinged upon these contrasting appearances. Police agents did not evoke anti-homeless ordinances in situations where the contrast between visible homelessness and prime spaces full of well-kept consumers was absent. None of the homeless persons reported being accused of panhandling or receiving anti-homeless ordinances outside of prime consumer spaces.

Moreover, some unemployed participants who looked like consumers – namely Vaughn and Tina – did not stand out in prime spaces and so dodged the excessive police attention that usually falls upon homeless persons. Vaughn, for instance, was the only participant who reported no police contact. He, however, had a consistent spot at a local shelter which gave him everyday clothes (he wore newer jeans, a ball cap, and a brand name t-shirt) and enabled him to keep them clean. I would not have approached him for an interview and would have assumed he was just waiting outside the mall after shopping had he not requested money from me. Tina similarly projected a strong middle-class consumer appearance – including sometimes accessorizing herself with Dolce and Gabana handbags. While she described encounters with police officers, these did not occur when she was panhandling or simply hanging out in public space. I also would not have asked Tina for an interview had she not first requested cash from me. Apparently, just as I would not have approached these persons for interviews because they did not meet the typical image of homelessness, police officers too overlooked their presence in prime spaces because they did not stand out.

The ability of persons like Tina and Vaughn to blend into consumers spaces demonstrates the importance these spaces play in the policing of homelessness. Proponents of the civic sanitation argument like Berti and Sommers (2010), Collins and Blomley (2003), Mitchell (1997, 2004), Feldman (2004), and Mosher (2002) contend that prime spaces are important because they attract homeless persons who seek aid from affluent pedestrians and because they contain the powerful business agents who demand police officers do something about homeless persons. The stories of participants further suggest that prime consumer spaces are essential to the policing of homelessness because they provide the contrasting background against which homeless persons stand out and can draw police attention.

In order to "see" any object a person must be able to distinguish the object from its surroundings (Merleau-Ponty, 2002). If the primary means of identifying the homeless is their appearance as unkempt or impoverished, this identification is easier in contexts where persons typically appear otherwise. As such, visibly homeless participants found that they quickly drew police attention in spaces of middle-class consumption and business traffic. Meanwhile, those homeless persons who could uphold the image of consumers did not stand out and were not as heavily policed. Enforcement of anti-homeless ordinances thus requires an identifiable other that is allegedly out of place among his or her surroundings. Prime consumer spaces provide the contrast between rich and poor, consumer and pauper, that police use to identify homeless persons and deploy anti-homeless ordinances like Edmonton's revised Public Places Bylaw (2009). As Darlene eloquently put is, in consumer spaces looking homeless means "you stand out more in the crowd" and so draw increased police attention.

Conclusion: Confirmation and Extension of the Civic Sanitation Argument

My observation that the appearance of visible homelessness in consumer space draws police attention aligns with the civic sanitation argument that anti-panhandling laws and other anti-homeless ordinances attempt to cleanse prime consumer spaces of visible reminders of poverty (e.g., Feldman, 2004; Martin, 2002; Mitchell, 1997, 2004; Mosher, 2002). This position challenges claims that these laws focus on the aggressive actions of panhandlers. Participants revealed that police officers accused them of panhandling and sanctioned them regardless of their actions. They did not have to be acting aggressively to receive fines or informal police sanctions. They did not even have to be panhandling. In fact, although the letter of the law focuses on behaviour, and despite repeated EPS cautions that they would not use the new bylaw to target all homeless persons (Hanon, 2009, n.p.; Kent, 2009, p. A), the enforcement of the revised Public Places Bylaw (2009) singled people out for police attention based on how they looked in certain spaces.

This appearance-based and spatially-underpinned policing complicates Gordon's (2006, 2011) argument that anti-panhandling laws are simply repackaged vagrancy statutes that punish those who reject wage labour. Many homeless persons held complex relationships to wage labour that officers did not attempt to verify. Moreover, some employed persons who were still visibly homeless continued to face police sanction, while some unemployed homeless persons who looked like consumers did not. The policing participants experienced thus did not revolve around their connection to, or their ability to engage in, wage labour.

The fact that participants received heavy policing when they stood out as homeless in the city's major spaces of outdoor consumption supports the civic sanitation argument. Indeed, the stories of participants like Darlene who were employed yet visibly homeless and so found themselves quickly expunged from consumer spaces, when contrasted with the stories of persons like Vaughn and Tina who dodged much police attention because they did not look homeless, confirm Feldman's (2004, p. 45) observation that:

> Whereas the begging prohibitions contained within vagrancy statutes historically centred on the problematic of idleness and the need to constitute a disciplined workforce ... the contemporary regulation of begging is oriented toward a different problem: the need to maintain a purified space of consumption. (Feldman, 2004, p. 45)

The policing of homelessness, then, is better understood as the policing of appearances in consumer spaces than the policing of wage labour relations.

The ability of some participants to avoid police attention by upholding consumer images further highlights the role of prime spaces in the policing of homeless. Scholars behind the civic sanitation argument have drawn attention to powerful business actors' attempts to use law enforcement to expel the homeless and aid gentrification in order to increase consumerism and profits (Berti & Sommers, 2010; Collins & Blomley, 2003; Mitchell, 2004). The stories of participants further demonstrate that since the policing of homelessness is based on identifying those who look homeless, this policing requires homeless persons to stand out from their surroundings. The policing of homelessness is concentrated in prime consumer spaces, in part, because these spaces provide the backdrop against which visibly homeless persons stand out and so draw police attention.

Because the policing of homelessness requires homeless persons to stand out in prime consumer spaces, it is essential, as proponents of the civic sanitation argument like Mitchell (2004) contend, that these spaces be reconstituted as inclusive spaces where all persons regardless of appearance are welcomed and treated equally. Laws like Edmonton's Public Places Bylaw (2009), and the police practices they enable, single out visibly homeless people as "out of place" and so dissolve this ideal equality. Fashioning inclusive public spaces therefore requires challenging these laws and the policing they enable. However, while the civic sanitation argument appropriately aims to create inclusive public spaces, several shortcomings within this position remain. In particular, those who advance this argument do not fully consider how police displace those who stand out in consumer spaces, how homeless persons' daily lives are structured through multiple spaces, and how experiences of policing differ within the homeless population. Creating fully inclusive public spaces requires attending to these gaps. It is to these issues that I now turn.

CHAPTER FIVE

FINED AND MOVED-OUT: DISPLACEMENT AND THE RACIALIZED POLICING OF MARGINALIZED AND PRIME SPACES

The policing of homelessness aims at visibly homeless persons who stand out in spaces of consumption. The civic sanitation argument – the claim that anti-homeless ordinances aid gentrification by expelling the poor – draws attention to the displacement of homeless persons from public spaces. This chapter moves beyond this argument and contends that civic sanitation requires marginalized spaces in which to place the homeless and that these spaces and the policing of homelessness are racialized. While anti-homeless efforts do indeed aim to drive the homeless out of certain spaces, the voices of participants document how policing displaces the homeless and how race shapes this displacement.

This discussion unfolds in four parts. First, I briefly review how the civic sanitation argument overlooks marginalized spaces and racialization. Second, I show how police use fines and move-outs to direct homeless persons into the marginalized spaces of the jail and the inner-city. Homeless persons are sent to these spaces because they allegedly manifest the criminal, violent, impoverished, and disorderly features of these spaces. Third, I argue that prime and marginalized spaces are racialized. Although both the jail and the inner-city already hold disproportionate numbers of Aboriginals, urban planning policies and the actions of police officers reinforce marginalized spaces as suitable places to confine Aboriginals. In so doing, these policing measures help maintain prime consumers spaces as ideally White spaces. Finally, I conclude by summarizing how the voices of the homeless help advance the civic sanitation argument and by highlighting how the differences among these voices complicate the call for inclusive city spaces.

Weaving Marginalized Spaces and Racialization into the Civic Sanitation Argument

The central claim of the civic sanitation argument is that anti-homeless ordinances truncate the ability of public spaces to become inclusive political spheres insofar as they attempt to attract consumers and business by "cleansing" public space of homeless persons who allegedly chase away customers and investment. Don Mitchell (1997, p. 305) conveys the general position of this argument and the language of sanitation that underpins it when he declares:

> In city after city concerned with ... making urban centres attractive to both footloose capital and footloose middle classes, politicians and managers of the new economy ... have turned to a legal remedy that seeks to cleanse the streets of those left behind by ... changes in the economy by simply erasing the spaces in which they must live. ... For this is what the new legal regime ... is outlawing: just those behaviours that poor people, and the homeless in particular, must do in public spaces of the city.

Mitchell (1997, 2004) goes on to declare that anti-homeless ordinances cleanse public space so thoroughly that they potentially eliminate the homeless. He says (1997, p. 310), "To the degree that laws can annihilate spaces for the homeless, they can annihilate the homeless themselves. When such anti-homeless laws cover all public space [as Edmonton's Public Places Bylaw does], then presumably the homeless will simply vanish." More temperate proponents of the civic sanitation argument like William O'Grady, Stephen Gaetz, and Kristy Buccieri (2011, p. 79) contend that because anti-homeless ordinances are more often enforced only in gentrifying areas, these laws do not eliminate the homeless but rather displace them and thereby reinforce the "boundaries between the homeless urban poor and others who use the city." O'Grady, Gaetz, and Buccieri (2011), however, do not fully discuss the spaces to which fines and other policing practices direct the street-involved. As such, it remains unclear where the "boundaries between the homeless ... and others who use the city" lie.

The civic sanitation argument accurately emphasizes the role of prime spaces in the policing of homelessness (Berti & Sommers, 2010; Collins & Blomley, 2003; Herbert & Brown, 2006), but neglects how every displacement sets the homeless into new spaces (Hogeveen & Freistadt, 2012). This neglect makes it seem like the homeless do, in fact, "simply vanish" (Mitchell, 1997, p. 310). How are homeless persons removed from prime consumer spaces? Where do they go? Julia Wardhaugh (1996; Wardhaugh & Jones, 1999) observes that homeless persons' everyday routines intersect with many different spaces, including marginalized spaces where poverty, crime, violence, and disorder are permitted (see also Feldman, 2004). Are Edmonton's homeless displaced to marginalized spaces? Which ones? Why are the homeless shunted to these areas? Attention to the multiple spaces that comprise homeless persons' everyday lives attends to these questions the civic sanitation argument leaves unaddressed.

Mitchell's (1997, 2004) position, alongside most other scholars who advance the civic sanitation argument like Damian Collins and Nicholas Blomley (2003), Janet Mosher (2002), Leonard Feldman (2004), and Mario Berti and Jeff Sommers (2010), also says little about differences among the persons who are pushed from prime consumer spaces. It is as if all homeless persons experience policing in the same way and so, regardless or characteristics like racial identity, equally disappear from public space. Other scholars like Elizabeth Comack (2012), Sherene Razack (2002a, 2002b), and Renisa Mawani (2002, 2005, 2012) have detailed how policing in Canada reinforces racial hierarchies and confines Aboriginal persons to marginalized spaces. Homelessness, however, is not the central focus of these authors. How does the policing of homelessness contribute to the racialization of space? Below I draw on the voices of Edmonton's homeless to address this important question.

The Jail and the Inner-City as Marginalized Spaces

By sketching how police practices displace them, participants' stories correct the civic sanitation argument's suggestion that the policing of homelessness causes all street-involved persons to "vanish" (Mitchell, 1997, p. 310). The homeless do not disappear but are instead redirected to spaces where their presence is permitted and where danger, crime, disorder, poverty, and violence are normalized. This displacement to marginalized spaces occurred through two police practices: fines and move-outs.

Fines as Spatial Controls

Homeless participants received many fines associated with different anti-homeless bylaws. The EPS claimed that the fines associated with anti-homeless ordinances such as Edmonton's Public Places Bylaw (2009) would deter homeless persons from the informal economy (Inspector Brian

Nowlan in Kent, 2009, p. B1). Participants' experiences, however, demonstrated that fines were not deterrents but instead became mechanisms of spatial exclusion (see also Herbert & Brown, 2006; O'Grady & Bright, 2002). Specifically, none of the persons who received fines for bylaw infractions said the penalties changed their behaviour. Financial penalties are lost on homeless persons who have insufficient money to pay them (O'Grady, Gaetz, & Buccieri, 2011). As Nick perceptively pointed out, "Well, ok, if you got no money in the first place, how are you going to pay the fine? That is a stupid circle." The stupidity of this circle meant that the homeless did not take the fines seriously. Mike explained casually of his panhandling tickets, "I got lots. I don't even know sometimes. I just throw them away because I am not going to pay them." Without adequate incomes to meet their more-pressing demands, none of the participants could pay the $250 fines issued through Edmonton's anti-panhandling provisions or other anti-homeless ordinances.[7] Instead, they inevitably served time in jail for nonpayment. As Tina explained, "You don't [pay]. You don't. And then you get a fail to appear, then you go to jail."

The voices of the homeless thus demonstrate that the fines attached to anti-homeless ordinances are not financial deterrents but rather means of displacing them from prime consumer spaces and temporarily confining them in jail cells. The jail and the prison, as Loic Wacquant (2009) observes, are, among other things, marginalized spaces used to segregate individuals constituted as disorderly, immoral, and criminal. The prison is a space where alleged criminals are shunted and violence, crime, and poverty are normalized features (Brooks, 2002; Morin, 2002). For many street-involved persons this marginalized space was simply a part of their routine. The homeless persons who received bylaw infractions talked about jail time as a regular course of events. Eli explained that getting fines means panhandlers simply do "a few days in jail and [it] gives them a break to come back and do the same thing all over again." While Bob confirmed that "nobody likes to be in jail," the nonchalant nature with which participants talked about jail, and Eli's declaration that jail gave the homeless "a break," convey that many saw this marginalized space an inevitable part of living on the streets.

The "cleansing" of prime spaces requires somewhere to put displaced persons. The experiences of the homeless demonstrate that the jail serves as one of the marginalized spaces in which impoverished persons who cannot uphold images of consumption are hidden from public view (Brooks, 2002; Wacquant, 2009).

---

[7] See O'Grady & Bright (2002), O'Grady, Gaetz and Buccieri (2011) and McNeil (2010) for similar findings in other Canadian cities.

Move-outs to the McCauley-Boyle Inner-City

Participants also reported that police officers often directly transported them out of prime consumer spaces and set them in different parts of the city, especially impoverished inner-city neighbourhoods. William King and Thomas Dunn (2004) refer to this practice as "dumping" or "police-initiated-transjurisdictional-transport." The term "move-out," however, is preferable for this study for two reasons. First, it avoids the suggestion that the persons escorted by police are waste. Second, some police move-outs participants spoke about did not usher them into new police jurisdictions but into marginalized neighbourhoods in the same jurisdiction.

Police have long used move-outs as informal measures to displace allegedly troublesome persons (Beckett & Herbert, 2009; Comack, 2012; King & Dunn, 2004). In Edmonton the 2005 "sweatbox" incident where the EPS collected nine Aboriginal homeless persons off Whyte Avenue, drove them around the city in a hot van for an hour and a half, and dropped them off in a deserted parking lot in a north-end community attests to the reality of this practice (Simons, 2007, p. B1). Indeed, during the disciplinary hearing into this event, EPS officials but admitted it was standard practice to "round up" homeless persons from Old Strathcona and Downtown. Such move-outs, however, were not supposed to leave persons in desolate parking lots. Rather, they were intended to drop the homeless off at inner-city shelters (Pierce, 2010, n.p.).

My interviews confirmed move-outs to inner-city shelters were the most common means of displacement. Outside of the "sweatbox" incident only one other participant mentioned being escorted to a deserted area where he had to walk back on his own. It was much more common for police move-outs to place participants in or around inner-city services, the majority of which are located in Edmonton's McCauley and Boyle Street neighbourhoods. Debrah, for instance, said police often pick her up from Whyte Avenue on the south side of the river and take her "all the way down to the Hope [Mission]" – an inner-city shelter in the McCauley-Boyle region. Russ relayed a similar occurrence. He said that when police saw him panhandling in Old Strathcona, "They [police officers] said they would take me up to the Hope Mission and drop me off there. And that is what they did." Darlene likewise explained that police frequently "pick [her] up" and "drop [her] off at Spady's," which is the colloquial term the street-involved use to refer to a shelter (the George Spady Centre) in the McCauley-Boyle region. The area was so familiar to homeless persons that participants who spent most of their time in Old Strathcona often referred to McCauley-Boyle simply as the "downtown" or the "north side."

Police have defended these move-outs to the "north side" as routine practices "of compassion" meant to help the homeless access services instead of face incarceration (see Pierce, 2010, n.p.). In most cases, however, the end result of these drop offs was not that homeless persons obtained services, but that they were simply displaced to the McCauley-Boyle region. Participants seldom utilized the agencies to which police transported them. In fact, while many individuals had been ushered to organizations in the McCauley and Boyle Street neighbourhoods by police, only one, Eli, reported that the end result was improved social services. Eli explained that he met the only social worker he was comfortable with through a "cop" who not only took him to an inner-city agency, but also "introduced" him to a worker who was from the same reserve. Eli's story, however, was exceptional because the officer took the time to link him with an appropriate social worker.

In most cases officers simply dropped homeless persons at agencies and assumed the organizations would do the rest. Rick described this more typical occurrence:

> They [the police] drive me to the Spady Centre. Drop me off and say, "We don't want to see you down here [Downtown] no more. You are banned off Jasper Avenue and you are not allowed to be down here no more panhandling because that is what you do all day."

The actions of the officers in this much more common case highlight that their dominant concern is to remove Rick from prime consumer space. The police officers did not make any effort to ensure Rick would benefit from, or remain at, the George Spady Centre. Rather, they simply left him with the direction that he is "banned off Jasper Avenue" because he panhandles. These parting words and actions stress where Rick ought not to be (the prime consumer space of Jasper Avenue), not what Rick ought to do to access help.

Very few participants, however, remained at the charities to which police transported them, which further suggests that move-outs are less about helping the homeless and more about displacing them to marginalized space. The homeless-serving agencies do not meet the needs, preferences, or desires of the entire street-involved population. Consequently, most homeless persons reported that as soon as officers left they exited the agencies, found themselves in the McCauley-Boyle inner-city, and returned to prime spaces.[8]

That many individuals did not remain inside the agencies police delivered them to must have been known by officers because they would eventually come back into contact with the same homeless persons. In fact,

---

[8] See Chapter 6 for a further discussion of participants' refusal to remain confined to marginalized spaces and the mobility patterns that result.

most people who experienced move-outs reported that it was often the same officers that repeatedly removed them from prime spaces. For example, Rick said, "They [the police officers who routinely escorted him to the shelter] know who I am and they call me by my first name." EPS officials even unwittingly admitted that they were aware move-outs did not result in service use for many homeless persons. Testifying at the disciplinary hearing for the "sweatbox" incident, the acting supervisor for the officers involved explained that members of the EPS did not formally record move-outs "because the drop-offs were so frequent" and "police would often have to transport the same individual two to three times in a single shift" (Pierce, 2010, n.p.). If police know that few homeless people use the inner-city agencies to which they are transported, then the move-out is less an effort to find homeless persons help than it is an act (intentional or otherwise) that displaces the homeless into the inner-city.

The McCauley and Boyle Street neighbourhoods to which the police displace the homeless are among the city's poorest and most crime ridden areas. Given the central role this marginalized space played in the lives of the homeless, I passed through the area several times. To be sure, the abutting communities boasts some successful, local, and independent stores that cater largely to immigrant communities (the area encompasses Little Italy and Chinatown). The neighbourhoods also contain several owner-occupied single-family dwellings that house residents who wish to improve the region's image (Kleiss, 2009, p. A15). Nevertheless, as I traversed the area I encountered many signs that constituted this region as marginalized space. For instance, travelling down the more developed streets I passed many drop-ins and soup kitchens with large lines of impoverished people waiting outside, several of the hopeful entrants sleeping on the sidewalk. Amongst these agencies are a mix of residential houses, rooming houses, and the markers of parasitic capitalism – bottle exchanges, pawn shops, high-interest money lenders, and a few weapons dealers (Hogeveen & Freistadt, 2013). Some of the streets are well-known sites for prostitution, and peering down alleyways past broken bottles and used needles I spied several groups drinking and interrupted a few open-air drug exchanges.

The homeless apparently "belong" in the region of McCauley-Boyle because this inner-city space reflects their poverty and their allegedly criminal, disorderly, and dangerous qualities. Homelessness, poverty, and crime are normalized features of the McCauley-Boyle streetscape and so police move-outs to this inner-city region are unlikely to result in major complaints. Rather, while visibly homeless persons stand out in consumer spaces, they blend into this setting. In fact, some participants reported that when they wanted to hang out in public space and be left alone by the police, they went to this area. Rick, for instance, explained how he sometimes retreated to the McCauley-Boyle inner-city. He said, "They [the police] just gave me a ticket and told me to leave. ... I went to, uh, I went to Boyle-McCauley. That area, you know? And I started hanging out there." After being harassed by police on Jasper Avenue, Rick headed for a community in which he would blend in and be ignored. It was the only area he knew of where he would not be harassed and could just "hang out."

Rick and others found sanctuary from constant police attention by hiding away in marginalized spaces where poverty was common. Indeed, I was reminded of how normalized poverty was in this space when, early in my fieldwork, I attempted to solicit an interview from an individual on an empty sidewalk in the Boyle Street neighbourhood. The individual looked homeless but I soon found out that he lived in a small suite above the stoop on which he sat. He was retired and poor, but he was neither homeless nor involved in the informal economy. This blunder reinforced the necessity of spatial contrasts in the policing of homeless. Just as the policing of homelessness hinges upon a contrast wherein the visibly homeless stand out in spaces of consumption, the displacement this policing completes requires a space in which the homeless are less likely to stand out and so unlikely to generate demands to yet-again remove them. Against a background of poverty, dilapidated housing, and social services, appearances associated with homelessness are more common and so police can displace the homeless to these areas with less public outcry.

Thus, like prisons, marginalized neighbourhoods become spaces of confinement that try to contain those stigmatized as criminal, violent, and disorderly (Wacquant, 2000, 2008). Although the borders of the McCauley-Boyle region are obviously more porous than prison walls, efforts to confine disadvantaged people to this marginalized space exist. Police tell the homeless they cannot be in prime consumer spaces but apparently allow and encourage them to live their lives in the public spaces of McCauley-Boyle. Additionally, the architecture of redevelopment and city planning attempts to solidify the boundaries between marginalized spaces and prime spaces (Hayward, 2004).

In Edmonton, for instance, the city is attempting to further concentrate poverty in the McCauley-Boyle inner-city. Although a portion of the Boyle neighbourhood closest to Downtown and the North Saskatchewan River is slated for gentrification to attract middle-class consumers (Granzow & Dean, 2007), a vast chunk of the Boyle neighbourhood has been set aside to house even more impoverished persons. Despite the fact that the area already contains a vast amount of social services (Granzow & Dean, 2007) and a hugely disproportionate rate of subsidized housing (Kleiss, 2010, p. A1), the City of Edmonton, in what it terms the "Boyle Renaissance," plans to build an additional 550 low-income housing units. This redevelopment includes a "mega-complex" that combines 150 units of affordable housing with rental spaces for social services (Kent, 2010, p. B3; McKay, Finnigan

& Associates, 2010; O'Donnell, 2012). Meanwhile, the redevelopment plan for the Downtown core, which shares part of its northern border with the McCauley-Boyle region, appears to solidify the divide between these two spaces. Along the portion of Downtown's 103A Avenue that marks the southern edge of the McCauley-Boyle region the Downtown redevelopment focuses on towers and large structures, including a new hockey arena (City of Edmonton, 2010a; Gregory, 2012; Sands & Kent, 2012). These huge, privately-owned structures turn their backs on the marginalized space of the inner-city, visually cut the area off from the adjacent prime space, and will likely employ private security to complicate any efforts marginalized individuals from McCauley-Boyle make to enter the Downtown core.

Confinement to marginalized inner-city space not only limits the public spaces available to homeless persons, it also presents several dangers. Homeless persons typically report that they feel safe in their familiar spaces because they know where to go to meet their daily needs and are protected by acquaintances (Beckett & Herbert, 2009). Removing homeless persons from their typical surroundings and their street families made them uncomfortable and exposed them to possible victimization, especially when they were placed into marginalized inner-city spaces rife with poverty and crime.

Participants confirmed the dangerousness of the McCauley-Boyle area. Many tried to avoid the area as much as possible. Stan described the constant threat of victimization he felt in the area:

> Fuck I lock my window, I put a blanket up and everything, I keep my lights on most of the time. People lurk around all night, they do man. People lurk around all night and day. … Oh robberies and everything man. There are just so many people that hang around in front of the liquor store, they are all alcoholics, they are all drug addicts, they are hanging out in front of the liquor store. You know what they do? … They wait for people to come out of the liquor store and even though they got one little bottle or six pack, they will grab it and fucking run.

Although Stan's rooming house was in McCauley, the dangers of the neighbourhood led him to remain on the street. He avoided the area, which he referred to as a "ghetto," as much as he could "because there is crime everywhere." Instead he spent most of his time Downtown where he felt safer. Keith also explained that he avoided the McCauley-Boyle area as a means of ensuring safety. When asked if he felt safe on the streets, he replied, "Oh yeah. I don't make a habit of going down around the Bissell or the Co-op [two adult drop-in centres in the McCauley and Boyle Street neighborhoods] or any place where there is high crime rate."

Marginalized spaces present dangers for everyone, including, and perhaps especially, the homeless. Stan and Keith were keenly aware of these dangers and tried to avoid them. Police, however, ignored these dangers and continued to usher homeless persons into the inner-city.

Racialized Policing Racializes Spaces

Participants, however, were not uniformly directed to dangerous marginalized spaces. Rather, race shaped police efforts to shunt them into the marginalized spaces necessary for the civic sanitation of prime spaces. This is not to say that only individuals who identified as Aboriginal were subject to practices of displacement. Police fined and moved-out both Aboriginal and non-Aboriginal participants, but these policing measures were clearly racialized insofar as police more readily applied fines and (especially) move-outs to homeless Aboriginals. It was much more difficult for Aboriginal persons to avoid these practices and remain within prime spaces. In fact, four visibly White males – Vaughn, Dan, Dean, and Jason – were the only persons who escaped both police fines and move-outs. Although three of these individuals were visibly homeless, engaged in behaviours similar to other homeless persons, and had consistent contact with police, none of them were forced into the marginalized spaces of the jail or the inner-city. Police apparently felt they did not so obviously belong in these dangerous spaces compared to their Aboriginal counterparts.

In contrast, Aboriginal homeless persons had more difficulty avoiding the fines that served to eventually confine them in jail cells. Three Aboriginal participants reported that they had not received fines related to anti-homeless ordinances – roughly the same proportion as White homeless persons who did not receive tickets. These three Aboriginals, however, had to take particular precautions to avoid fines. One always busked to make money in the informal economy (which arguably helped him avoid being accused of panhandling) and when he was not busking spent most of his time in the McCauley and Boyle Street neighbourhoods. Meanwhile, the other two always pleaded or agreed to be taken to local shelters instead of fined. In contrast, the four White men who escaped fines associated with anti-homeless ordinances did not have to leave prime spaces or limit their time within them.

That homeless Aboriginals had greater difficulty escaping the fines that led to jail is unfortunate but not surprising. Canadian prisons are highly racialized spaces. Although only 3.1 percent of Canadians adults self-identified as Aboriginal in the 2006 Census, 18 percent of adults admitted into provincial or territorial custody in 2007/2008 were Aboriginal (Perreault, 2009). This overrepresentation is all the more apparent in the local context. In Alberta, the percentage of Aboriginal persons in provincial custody or remand (the latter of which is where persons often spend time for unpaid bylaw tickets) is seven times their percentage in the provincial population (Perreault, 2009). Les Samuelson and Patricia Monture-Angus (2002), alongside Renisa Mawani and David Sealy (2011), observe that mass incarceration is an extension of ongoing colonial efforts to segregate an Aboriginal population constituted as a threat to the White settlement and domination of valuable spaces. Police actions that make it more difficult for Aboriginal homeless persons to avoid confinement in jail ought to be read as continuations of these practices. Homeless Aboriginals in prime spaces, by being both poor and having a non-White racial identity, threaten the White domination of prime spaces and so face greater chances of fines and eventual segregation from primes spaces through carceral confinement.

Move-outs were an even more obviously racialized police practice. The busker who spent most of his time in the McCauley and Boyle Street neighborhoods was the only Aboriginal participant who reported that police had not ushered him into the inner-city. This was arguably because he already spent most of his time there. All other Aboriginal participants explained that police frequently removed them from Downtown or Old Strathcona and dropped them off in the inner-city at or near social services. In contrast, only one White homeless man, Rick, reported that police ushered him to shelters in the McCauley-Boyle inner-city. Rick, however, often wanted to go to these agencies. Describing one move-out to an inner-city shelter, he said, "I would have went regardless of whether they took me or not. I don't mind going to the Spady's ... or Hope Mission just to get off the streets, take a break once in a while." Although Rick typically exited the agencies soon after police left, he "didn't mind" being in the shelters or the space of McCauley-Boyle "once in a while." His move-outs, then, put him in spaces that were not large inconveniences to him.

While police seemed attuned to Rick's preferences, they paid less attention to the wishes of homeless Aboriginals. Most Aboriginal participants did not want to go to the inner-city shelters but police took them anyways. Police often allowed White homeless persons to stay within the general proximity of prime consumer spaces, but Aboriginal participants were quickly ushered into the McCauley-Boyle inner-city.

The following two stories are representative of the differential police treatment of Aboriginal and White homeless participants in prime consumer spaces. The first involves Jason, a White homeless man, whom the police allow to stay in the Whyte Avenue area:

I said [to the officers waking him up in an alley behind Whyte Avenue], "Guys give me a break, at least let me sleep a couple hours". He said, "I would if I could, but I can't. If we get a complaint, it goes on our system, we have to do something about it and chase you out." He says,

"I will tell you what though, between you and me, go a couple blocks that way away from Whyte and find a place to go to sleep."

The second involves Stan, an Aboriginal man, who tries to occupy the same space.

I went to Whyte Avenue. I was panhandling and they [the police] say, "You panhandling? … What are you doing here? You can't be sitting around here. You know what, we think you are panhandling. … Where are you from?" I say, "I am homeless." They say, "Well we are going to drive you to the Hope Mission."

Jason is a White homeless male sleeping in public space. When police received a complaint about his presence, they allowed him to remain in the area and find rest nearby, so long as he was not directly along Whyte Avenue. In contrast, it is not clear that police received any complaints about Stan yet they nevertheless accused him of panhandling and told him he could not be in the area. As a homeless Aboriginal man, officers rapidly identified Stan as "out of place" in the prime consumer space of Whyte Avenue and sent him to the space where he apparently belongs – the McCauley-Boyle neighbourhood (Hogeveen & Freistadt, 2013).

Samuelson and Monture-Angus (2002), alongside other scholars like Razack (2002a, 2002b), contend that stereotypes perpetuated by colonial processes continue to encourage many non-Aboriginal persons to conceive Aboriginal peoples as lazy, drunkards, disorderly, criminal, and dangerous. Razack demonstrates that such constructions justify the confinement of Aboriginal persons to marginalized spaces rife with poverty, drinking, and crime. The McCauley-Boyle region clearly meets this image of marginalized space as dangerous and so appears as a legitimate container for such negatively stereotyped Aboriginals. Indeed, inner-cities are already spaces in which Aboriginal people are overrepresented (La Prairie, 2002).

In Edmonton, while only 1.2 percent of housed residents listed an Aboriginal background as their single origin in the 2001 Census, the percentage of respondents who identified with these backgrounds in the McCauley and Boyle Street neighbourhoods were 10.4 percent and 5.6 percent respectively (City of Edmonton 2005a, 2005b, 2005c). Both McCauley and Boyle Street are also home to many other ethnicities, but the region's designation as a space of Aboriginality is obvious and increasing. In particular, many of the low-income units and social services spaces being built as part of the Boyle Renaissance are reserved for Aboriginal clients and organization. Moreover, the middle of the Boyle Renaissance redevelopment will feature an urban park that designers claim is inspired by Aboriginal symbols (McKay Finnigan & Associates, 2010).

Female Aboriginals were even more likely to be associated with, and transported to, the marginalized and racialized inner-city regardless of their wishes. Debrah, for instance, said that she preferred to stay in Old Strathcona. She explained, "when I go down that way [into the inner-city], I get really mad." She once lived in McCauley but now felt the area was very unsafe for her. She still held a bad reputation among some people in the neighbourhood. People on the "north side," Dehrah explained, continued to call her by her old street name – "Wild Child" – and this reputation meant that she faced a high likelihood of victimization when she returned to the area. Nevertheless, despite the fact that going into the neighbourhood was particularly dangerous for her and put her in touch with old contacts she wanted to avoid, police regularly transported her to the inner-city and dropped her off at the Hope Mission.

In contrast, police never escorted her boyfriend Kyle, who was also homeless but White, to the shelters because he preferred not to go.

Debrah: They [police] give us a ticket or then they drive us downtown. …

Kyle: No, not me, I don't go downtown …. [Police] give us a ticket and tell us to go on our own. … I tell them no [when they say they are taking him to the inner-city] …

Debrah: Well they take me downtown. I got to go to Hope Mission.

Although neither Debrah nor Kyle want to go near inner-city shelters and both would prefer to remain together, police routinely usher Debrah out of Old Strathcona and place her outside the Hope Mission in the McCauley-Boyle region. Kyle purportedly simply tells officers "no" and his request is granted, while Debrah is always removed from the prime consumer space of Whyte Avenue. The move-outs are so common for Debrah that she no longer tries to protest. She sees her removal as dangerous but inevitable and simply explains that she has "got to go." The police officers seem to pay less attention to her desires and safety than they do to the preferences of her White male partner.

Debrah's experiences highlight how this racialized policing is particularly salient among Aboriginal women. Razack (2002a) and Mawani (2002) observe that police and colonial administrators often construct Aboriginal women as dirty, disorderly, criminal, and/or (sexually) immoral and so view these women as most appropriately belonging in spaces marred with the same stigmas. Debrah and all other homeless Aboriginal females were quickly escorted out of prime consumer spaces and ushered into the McCauley-Boyle region. Police apparently feel as though they, as disadvantaged Aboriginal women, belong in the marginalized inner-city space of crime, disorder, and violence.

While identity groups ought to have their own spaces to celebrate their differences, Comack (2012) reveals that constituting the inner-city as a space of Aboriginality perpetuates racialized policing and strengthens the borders surrounding racialized spaces. Confining Aboriginal people in marginalized spaces reinforces perceptions that Aboriginal people share the dangerous characteristics of these spaces (Razack, 2002a). In turn, because Aboriginal people are confined to predominately marginalized and dangerous spaces, others see them as greater threats within and outside these spaces and so they are more heavily policed. Confining Aboriginal persons to marginalized spaces can thus perpetuate the negative stereotypes some White persons hold about Aboriginals (Comack, 2012). This, in turn, can lead some White persons to conclude that they are superior and that they own, and must protect, prime spaces. These practices racialize both prime and marginalized spaces such that prime spaces appear as ideally White spaces and marginalized spaces appear as Aboriginal or non-White (Razack, 2002a, 2002b).

Participants were not immune from processes that perpetuate the racialization of prime and marginalized spaces. Police officers' displacement of Aboriginal homeless persons from prime spaces, coupled with their greater permissiveness toward White homeless men, resonated among some street-involved circles. Specifically, some of the White homeless men whom officers permitted to stay in the prime space of Old Strathcona began to see the area as properly belonging to them and other White people.

Dan, a White recycler who works the alleys behind Whyte Avenue, for instance, demonstrated how he, and the EPS, tied Aboriginality to crime and marginalized "north side" space. He declared:

Yeah, we [his street associates who are White bottle pickers] are probably some of the better guys in Edmonton. On the south side, you don't get the rowdies. But we are becoming a minority now. We are getting taken over by the Natives. There is getting to be too many of them. ... They are gonna form a union and take over our routes ... I have informed the police already of it and told them what is coming down. They said, "Don't worry about it, we know who all the north side guys are, and if we see too many of them over here causing problems, we will send them back where they come from." ... They know we don't hurt anybody. We don't break into peoples' garages and stuff like that. But those people will, I know they will.

Dan viewed "north side" Aboriginals as the source of most problems in the Old Strathcona neighbourhood. To him, "those people" resorted to crime, unjustifiably invaded his bottle-picking territory, and did not belong in his neighbourhood. He had good relationships with local police officers and when he expressed concern to them about the "Natives" they too apparently felt these homeless Aboriginals did not belong in Old Strathcona and promised to "send them back where they came from." The marginalized "north side" space of McCauley-Boyle was, according to the police and Dan, a space of Aboriginality and Aboriginals were criminals who belonged in that crime-ridden space. Meanwhile, the prime space of Old Strathcona and Whyte Avenue were ideally White spaces and any ills within this spaces were apparently the cause of Aboriginal outsiders.

Conclusion: Inclusive Public Space Must Address the Marginalized Spaces and Racial Hierarchies that Enable Displacement

While the civic sanitation argument highlights how anti-homeless ordinances hope to displace homeless persons from prime spaces, the voices of the homeless draw attention to the marginalized spaces that enable this displacement and how this displacement is racialized. As civic sanitation proponents like Mitchell (2004) contend, urban redevelopment attempts to construct prime public spaces of unfettered investment, consumption, and leisure. Doing so requires removing manifestations of poverty and inequality, like homeless persons, so that business investment and consumerism remain unquestioned (Berti & Sommers, 2010; Collins & Blomley, 2003; Feldman, 2004; Herbert & Brown, 2006; Mitchell, 1997, 2004; Mosher, 2002; O'Grady, Gaetz & Buccieri, 2011). Homeless persons, however, do not simply vanish (cf. Mitchell, 1997). Rather, their experiences highlight that removing them from prime spaces entails displacing them to marginalized spaces where their presence is permitted and their visible poverty or racial identity stand out less.

The jail and the inner-city comprise the marginalized and racialized spaces set aside to confine the homeless. Policing shunts homeless persons to these dangerous spaces through fines and move-outs. Both these policing practices, however, are highly racialized. Aboriginal homeless persons had greater difficulty avoiding fines and were much more likely to be moved-out to the McCauley-Boyle inner-city. Both the jail and the inner-city are already racialized spaces wherein Aboriginal persons ostensibly belong. Police-initiated move-outs and fines further racialize prime and marginalized spaces and help solidify the boundaries between these spaces. In so doing, these racialized police practices reflect Razack's (2002a) argument that racialized policing reproduces a long-standing hierarchy in which White persons can more easily enjoy, and exist within, prime spaces, while Aboriginal persons are more readily confined to dangerous marginalized spaces. Confining homeless persons, especially Aboriginal homeless persons, to marginalized spaces allows prime spaces to establish themselves as devoid of poverty, inequality, and racism without having to address the underlying causes of these issues. As such, the status quo of consumption, investment, and White ownership in prime spaces can continue unabated.

Those behind the civic sanitation argument like Mitchell (1997, 2004), Mosher (2002), and Feldman (2004) contend that removing homeless persons from public spaces is an exclusionary act that cuts off encounters with the poor and limits the ability of public spaces to become inclusive spheres for political change. The voices of the homeless demonstrate that they are excluded from certain public spaces but not all. Moreover, the stories of the homeless reveal that not all individuals face the same exclusionary practices in equal measure. Calls for public spaces that include the homeless must be attuned to the differences among the homeless population and the role of marginalized spaces in the policing of homelessness. While proponents of the civic sanitation argument like Mitchell (2004) stress homeless persons' rights to consumer spaces (see Blomley, 2011), promoting an inclusive city requires not only admonishing the "cleansing" of prime spaces but also acknowledging and addressing racism and the creation of marginalized and racialized spaces where poverty, addictions, Aboriginality, homelessness, crime, and violence are concentrated.

CHAPTER SIX

RETURNING HOME AND MOVING-ALONG: THE POLITICS OF RACIALIZED HOMELESS MOBILITY PATTERNS

Talking about displacement begins to engage the topic of mobility insofar as policing moves the homeless from one place to another. Current discussions of displacement or civic sanitation focus on gentrifying prime spaces and so overlook mobility in and of itself (Hannam, Sheller & Urry, 2006). This chapter attends to the theme of mobility and focuses on homeless persons' movements between and within prime and marginalized spaces. I argue that homeless persons return to the prime spaces they consider home and are constantly moved-along within those spaces, which creates circulatory mobility patterns that advance the interests of businesses, perpetuate the policing of homelessness, and reinforce racial hierarchies.

This argument draws on Tim Cresswell's (2006, 2010, 2012) desire to sketch the "politics of mobility" (see also Hannam, Sheller & Urry, 2006) and on Todd Gordon's (2006) observation that policing has (at least sometimes) protected the interests of the powerful. Examining the mobility patterns that shape homeless persons' everyday lives addresses issues overlooked by Sherene Razack's (2002a, 2002b) and Nicholas Blomley's (2007, 2011, 2012) discussions of mobility and the policing of space. Razack's (2002b) analysis of how policing racializes space assumes successful confinement and does not address what persons do once shunted to marginalized spaces. Blomley's (2007, 2011, 2012) argument, on the other hand, centralizes mobility but his discussion remains abstract insofar as it is removed from the lives of the homeless. While he argues that proponents of anti-homeless ordinances defend these laws through an egalitarian and apolitical police logic of pedestrianism that glorifies sidewalk mobility flows, I document how mobility patterns play out in the lives of the homeless and serve particular interests.

This chapter takes four turns. First, I review Blomley's (2007, 2011, 2012) pedestrianism argument and Razack's (2002a) discussion of how mobility factors into the racialization space. I draw on scholarship from the "mobilities turn" in the social sciences (see Hannam, Sheller & Urry, 2006) to demonstrate the need to examine what homeless persons do once displaced, the patterns of mobility the policing of homelessness produces, how these patterns are racialized, and the interests that these mobilities serve.

Second, I outline participants' mobility patterns. I discuss how many homeless persons viewed prime spaces as their home and so refused to remain in marginalized spaces. The homeless continually returned to prime spaces where they were repeatedly moved-along by police agents and/or used constant movement to blend-in and avoid ejection.

Third, I use the stories of participants to sketch the politics of these mobility patterns. I show how the mobilities produced through the policing of homelessness commodify rest and protect the interests of businesses, keep police agents employed, and reproduce colonial constructions of prime spaces as particularly fit for White settlement.

I conclude by discussing how these mobility patterns continue to truncate the potential of prime spaces to become spaces for reform by reducing the chances of sustained contact with homeless persons, especially street-involved Aboriginals. I contend that public spaces with transformative potential cannot be simply spaces of mobility or passage but instead must become spaces in which all persons, regardless of wealth, housing, or racial identity, can settle.

Unaddressed Questions about Homeless Mobility

Blomley's (2007, 2011, 2012) pedestrianism argument is the most explicit attempt to link the topic of mobility with the policing of homelessness. For Blomley anti-homeless ordinances, and the arguments used to defend them, manifest a logic of pedestrianism that contends that the sidewalk is first and foremost a space to ensure the free passage of all persons. After examining a litany of municipal laws and the arguments of civil engineers, politicians, and judges, Blomley concludes that pedestrianism underpins bylaws concerning public space. He notes that municipal law treats diverse topics — including bus-stops, panhandlers, and sidewalk cafes — as potential obstructions to mobility that ought to be policed. Because spatial regulations apply to all these different things, some of which are implements of businesses, Blomley (2011, p. 72) concludes that pedestrianism is an egalitarian and apolitical logic insofar as "the powerful and dispossessed are in theory, and often in practice, equally subject to its effects." As such, Blomley (2011, 2012) contends that attempts to identify a politics behind anti-homeless ordinances (including claims that such laws serve the interests of consumer capitalism through the civic sanitation of prime spaces) are limited because the egalitarianism of pedestrianism allows these laws to sidestep charges that they protect the interests of some and not others.

Blomley's analysis, however, does not document how the mobility glorified by those who support anti-homeless ordinances plays out on the sidewalk or in the lives of the homeless. He shows how concerns over mobility dominate the boardroom, the legislature, and the courthouse, but not how they unfold on the street. As such, many questions remain about how mobility and the policing of homelessness intersect on the ground. Does the logic of pedestrianism evident in the arguments used to support anti-homeless ordinances manifest itself in the policing of homelessness? How does policing shape homeless persons' patterns of mobility?

Blomley's position that pedestrianism is egalitarian and apolitical also generates important questions. Although there are laws about the location of businesses and their implements or customers, are these laws as rigorously enforced as anti-homeless ordinances or do police agents only view certain obstructive people as problems? Does policing, as it unfolds on the ground, equally demand mobility of all who use public space? What about differences in the mobility patterns among the homeless, especially those differences stemming from racialized policing practices? If mobility is not policed in the egalitarian ways Blomley suggests, whose interests are served through the homeless mobility patterns policing generates?

Urban policing has a history of sometimes serving the interests of capital (Gordon, 2006, 2012; Neocleous, 2000, 2006) and the "mobility turn" in the social sciences demonstrates the importance of tracing the "politics of mobility" (Cresswell, 2006, 2010, 2012; Hannam, Sheller & Urry, 2006). Blomley's (2011, p. 101) reluctance to discuss the politics of enforced mobility on the sidewalk stems from his conception of pedestrianism as an abstract logic that underpins municipal law writ large and glorifies travel from "point A to point B." Cresswell (2010, p. 554), however, observes that mobility "is about more than getting from A to B" and should not be discussed as an abstract category (see also Cresswell, 2006, 2012; Hannam, Sheller & Urry, 2006). Rather, mobility should be examined as specific and meaningful movements. These movements are caught up in a politics because they grant or deny privileges, expose persons to different dangers or goods, and are produced or denied through socio-economic processes and powerful actors. Moreover, these movements comprise part of someone's lived experience and so analyses of mobility must recognize that there are important differences in the experiences of movement among and between groups – some people are allowed to move in certain spaces, others are permitted to move in only other spaces, and others still are denied movement (Cresswell, 2006; Hannam, Sheller & Urry, 2006).

I address issues overlooked in Blomley's discussion of mobility as an abstract category by focusing on the everyday mobility patterns of homeless persons, how they differ among the homeless, and how they connect to policing. Documenting the specific patterns of mobility that shape individuals' lived experiences includes examining how specific laws and practices encourage these mobilities instead of detailing the glorification of mobility among a range of municipal laws. Blomley correctly demonstrates that things concerning business owners are also subject to bylaws that encourage movement from point A to point B, but he does not consider the drastic differences among these laws. Bylaws concerning businesses regulate where things associated with the business (like sandwich boards, sidewalk cafes, and newsstands) must be positioned so as to minimize traffic obstruction in public spaces. In contrast, anti-homeless ordinances, like Edmonton's revised Public Places Bylaw (2009), do not set aside spaces in which panhandling can legally occur (Mitchell, 2004). It is thus pertinent to investigate if and how pedestrianism plays out in the policing of homelessness instead of interrogating its presence in municipal law writ large.

Blomley (2011) is aware of the importance of such a project insofar as he encourages other scholars to consider ways to challenge the police logic of pedestrianism behind anti-homeless ordinances. This chapter takes initial steps toward this challenge by discussing how the policing of homelessness creates specific mobility patterns in the lives of the homeless, how racialized policing shapes these patterns, the consequences these mobilities have, and the interests they serve. Doing so reveals the practices and politics behind the policing of homelessness. Without identifying these things it remains unclear what scholars who hope to overturn the police logic of pedestrianism that underpins anti-homeless ordinances ought to challenge.

Examining mobility in the lives of the homeless also contributes to discussions of racialized displacement. While Blomley's focus does not include considerations of how race intersects with policing and mobility, existing analysis of how policing racializes spaces do not give a full account of mobility. Razack (2002b), for example, explicitly acknowledges that she and other scholars examining the racialization of space do not consider how individuals might resist confinement to marginalized spaces. Rather, the focus is on how policing creates a unidirectional flow of racialized persons to marginalized spaces. What happens to individuals once police shunt them into marginalized spaces remains unclear. As such, the policing that helps racialize spaces appears to be completely successful at confining certain persons to marginalized spaces and stripping them of any ability to move. Razack (2002a, 2002b), for instance, contends that policing confines Aboriginal persons to marginalized spaces and entirely reduces their mobility and therefore constitutes them as less powerful than White persons who can pass freely in and out of spaces of their choosing. However, without examining the experiences of homeless persons, it is not obvious that they remain confined to marginalized spaces. What do homeless persons do once ushered into marginalized spaces? How might they counter efforts to confine them to spaces like the jail or the inner-city?

Razack's suggestion that more mobility aligns with privilege and power also needs refinement. As Christine Jocoy and Vincent Del Casino (2010, p. 147) remark, "Mobility and immobility are each generative of both power and powerlessness." Whether mobility reflects or produces higher social standing depends on the sources and effects of the movements under consideration. Some movements can force people into disadvantaged places or conditions, while not having to move can reflect privilege. It is misleading to assume that greater mobility equates to greater privilege (Cresswell, 2012). Drawing conclusions about who benefits from mobility necessitates outlining the different patterns of mobility among subjects, the reasons for movement, the consequences of movements for different actors, and the interests that these mobilities serve.

Homeless Persons Return to and Circulate Within Prime Spaces

Participants' voices fill in the blanks required to consider how the policing of homelessness connects to the patterns and politics of mobility. First of all, the stories of the homeless demonstrate that their movements do not end once they are displaced to marginalized and racialized spaces. Move-outs and fines attempt to confine the homeless to the jail or the inner-city, but these displacements are temporally limited. While the EPS repeatedly justifies the use of fines or move-outs, it is also apparently aware of the temporal limits of its efforts to confine the homeless. For instance, in a Community Crime Update video that warns viewers about panhandling, Edmonton police officers load alleged panhandlers into a van and proudly declare, "Now we are going to get these guys out of the area, at least for the weekend" (EPSVideoOnline, 2011). It is unclear whether the officers plan to take the alleged panhandlers to jail or to some other city space. It is clear, however, that the officers recognize the limited temporality of their efforts. The "solution" they offer by ushering the homeless into marginalized space is limited to a few days over "the weekend." Participants' stories confirmed that regardless of the marginalized space to which policing efforts shunted them, they eventually returned to the prime spaces in which they worked.

In fact, it is well documented that most homeless persons circulate between the streets and the prison system (Gowan, 2002; Thomson, Knutson, deKoning, Grekul & Fawcett, 2010). Among participants, this pattern of mobility included frequent movements between jail and the prime spaces in which police penalized their lifestyles. In particular, all participants who received tickets associated with Edmonton's revised Public Places Bylaw (2009) or other anti-homeless ordinances spent repeated short durations in jail for non-payment. Tina explained that the jail time to settle a quality of life bylaw infraction was "maybe two days." Time spent in jail, however, does nothing to address homelessness or involvement in the informal economy. In fact, time served for non-payment of bylaw tickets typically occurs in remand where services for prisoners are dismal (Weinrath, 2009). Consequently, many homeless persons who spend time in jail simply return to the streets after their release (Gowan, 2009).

Participants confirmed that when they served time for non-payment they did not receive services to ensure they would eventually enter into healthy and stable housing conditions. Kyle's experiences reflect the typical manner in which homeless persons were dismissed from the criminal justice system. When asked what happens when he is repeatedly released from jail and if there were efforts to link him with Housing First programming, halfway houses, or addictions services, he declared, "No. Nope. All they say is 'Get out. You are on your own. Go.' … Get out. … That is it." Without links to sufficient resources to help them find adequate housing or address their reasons for involvement in the informal economy, homeless persons who spent time in jail for tickets understandably found themselves back on the streets and trying to earn cash by busking, panhandling, and bottle picking within Edmonton's prime consumer spaces. This, however, simply draws them back into the sights of police officers, who then re-process them into the criminal justice system. Homelessness and the criminal justice system thus become mutually reinforcing. Jail time erodes the likelihood of securing housing by straining family ties, jeopardizing employment prospects, and dissolving housing references, while street life increases the likelihood of criminal justice contact (Gowan, 2002). Many homeless persons threfore find themselves whirling between the prime spaces in which they meet their needs and the jail cells that punish them for meeting their needs in prime spaces.

Participants also explained that efforts to confine them to the inner-city were limited. Homeless persons escorted to the McCauley-Boyle region soon returned to their familiar streetscapes. For example, after Darlene explained that police routinely picked her up from Downtown or Whyte Avenue and dropped her off at the George Spady Centre, she laughingly added, "And I go right back." Stan likewise reported that after police escort him out of Old Strathcona he simply turns around and returns. He chuckled, "You go to Whyte Avenue and panhandle, they [the police] throw you in the van and take you downtown and say, 'Don't come back.' …. Oh yeah, I go back there again." Indeed, all the street-involved persons I spoke with said that anytime they were moved-out of an area, they simply waited a brief period of time and then returned to the spaces from which police officers had ejected them.

Both the EPS and the homeless acknowledged that efforts to expel them from prime spaces were temporary and so short-sighted. As participants described how they returned from the inner-city to prime spaces they commonly laughed at the absurdity of such efforts. Both police authorities and homeless persons referred to the move-outs as a "game." Edmonton Police Staff Sergeant Doug Fedechko, for instance, explained during the disciplinary hearing into the "sweatbox" incident that homeless persons who police dropped off at shelters "often joked, calling it a game. … They would laugh and say, 'See you in a few hours,' when they were dropped off" (Pierce, 2010, n.p.). Of course, once the homeless returned to prime consumer spaces "in a few hours," police would simply pick them up again and drop them back off in the McCauley-Boyle region. Move-outs thus generated a circulatory pattern wherein the homeless would continually find themselves removed from prime spaces to marginalized spaces only to move back to prime spaces again.

Homeless Persons Moved-Along to Blend into Prime Spaces

When homeless persons were in prime consumer spaces, if they were not once again ushered into marginalized spaces, they soon faced demands to "move-along." Whereas move-outs physically escort homeless people to a new location, move-alongs involve commands to go elsewhere. Move-alongs are longstanding informal police responses to the homeless (Dean & Melrose, 1999; Golub, Johnson, Taylor, & Eterno, 2003, p. 690; Hermer, 1997; O'Grady, Gaetz & Buccieri, 2011). In spaces of tourism and consumption where pedestrian flows are the norm, stasis marks the homeless as "out of place" and draws police attention (Feldman, 2004). Police agents, in turn, attempt to rid areas of these highly visible markers of poverty by telling them to engage in some sort of movement and go elsewhere.

Move-alongs were the most common responses participants received from police agents. Nick, for instance, described one occasion where his stasis drew attention and led a police officer to forcefully demand that he move-along.

Well, when I was on the street, you see that [restaurant], that is where I slept. … I got kicked out of the LRT [Light Rail Transit], so I come up here, I had a towel over me, and I put my hat out at that time. And people were throwing change into it. I was sleeping hey. I hadn't slept. And this cop walked up and kicked me in the head. Literally kicked me in the head to wake me up. ... "Get moving."

The instructions of the officer demonstrate the importance of mobility. Despite the fact that Nick has a physical disability and cannot easily move, the officers were not pleased with his stasis and literally demanded that he "get moving."

Tina explained that security guards also commonly insist that the homeless leave an area. She described one such instance where she was told she could not be in a certain locale and so had to go elsewhere:

Well there are the couple guards from the hotel. They are just anal. They are like, "Get off the property [shrieking]. Get off here right now." And he runs out there with his flashlight in my face and is just really rude. You know, they could tell me to leave. ... They don't have to yell at me.

Dean likewise said security often chased him off public property, albeit in a more polite fashion. He nonchalantly explained that when he is panhandling, "They usually just come out and tell you that you can't be doing that here."

Like most other participants, Nick, Tina and Dean were continually told to leave and go elsewhere if they panhandled or loitered in one stop for any period of time. Their days were filled with demands to move-along. They were not allowed to be static elements of prime spaces. Indeed, if the homeless keep moving they are better able to blend into busy consumer spaces and so draw fewer complaints (Feldman, 2004; Jocoy & Del Casino, 2010). The enforcement of anti-homeless ordinances thus helps establish mobility as the norm in consumer spaces (Feldman, 2004).

Given the frequency with which homeless persons are told to "get moving" by security or police officers, it is perhaps unsurprising that many set themselves in aimless motion to avoid demands to move-along in the first place (Jocoy & Del Casino, 2010). Keith, for instance, explained that to avoid harassment from policing agents he spent any time on the street where he did not have newspapers to sell pacing up and down Jasper Avenue. He stated:

I really don't stand in one spot when I am on the street and I got no papers. I migrate back and forth. ... That way you are not blamed for anything. You know? People don't see you standing there.

Stan also explained that to avoid police agents he travels around the city on transit. He said:

> I know where to go to be left alone … I travel around. Bus drivers give me free rides. I say I am homeless, can you donate a ride? They say, "Where are you going?" I say, "I am going to the mall."

Marie likewise stated that she constantly moved around while panhandling to avoid upsetting security guards. She explained, "I keep walking. I could be one minute at one place and I could be six blocks over the next minute. … I am not standing in front of stores, I am moving … and … they [security] respect that."

Keith, Stan, and Marie adopt practices of mobility in order to blend into the busy setting of prime urban spaces and avoid being singled out by police agents. Keith does not want to be accused of troublemaking and so walks tirelessly about the streets unless he has newspapers that justify his stasis. Stan seeks refuge in different city malls and although security officers seldom allow him to remain in the mall, the long meandering bus trips from one mall to the next allow him to avoid encounters with police on the streets.[9] Marie tries to employ a mobile form of panhandling so security guards do not see her standing in front of businesses and chase her away. By remaining in constant motion homeless persons can avoid being shooed into marginalized spaces. Mobility allows them to temporarily blend-in with the busy urban setting and thus makes them less visible in prime spaces.

"I Am Not Going to Leave the Ave": Home for Homeless Persons

These mobility patterns of circulation within, or return to, prime spaces reflect the strong attachments homeless persons have to particular spaces and the deep subjective meaning they give to these spaces. Homeless persons have social, practical, and symbolic connections to specific locales (Beckett & Herbert, 2009; Mayers, 2001; Pratt, Gau & Franklin, 2011; Tanner, 2009). Like everyone else, homeless persons rely on familiar time-space patterns and local networks to meet their daily needs. Over time, they come to view the spaces in which they meet their needs as their own (Beckett & Herbert, 2009).

Participants thus identified the streets of prime spaces as their homes. Keith, for instance, explained that his home was the area in which he slept

---

[9] Jocoy and Del Casino (2010) similarly found that homeless persons in Long Beach, California took aimless walks and bus trips in an effort to avoid harassment.

and sold newspapers. When asked what he considered his home, he replied, "Right here, Jasper Avenue." Although Keith was without shelter and slept in alleyways Downtown, his home was the space in which he struggled to meet his daily needs. He relied on the familiar pattern of office workers going to and from work to sell his newspapers at prominent intersections along Jasper Avenue. He claimed a niche in a local alleyway as his own spot – referring to it possessively as "my cubbyhole," a sort of self-declared semi-private bedroom where he was hidden from view within his Downtown home. Another participant, Eli, also poignantly identified the streets as his home. When asked what he considered home he explained, "We [panhandlers in general] drink to survive and we eat to survive, but we live out here and we can't get inside, we are scared to be, we are claustrophobic." Eli not only affirmed that the streets were his home, he could not imagine living anywhere else. After approximately 40 years on the street he was "claustrophobic" and scared of the idea of being indoors. Over time the gentrifying space of Old Strathcona became the only place he was comfortable doing all the other things housed people do in their private dwellings.

Police agents and business leaders who support efforts to displace the homeless to marginalized spaces underestimate the strong attachments homeless persons give to specific prime spaces. As Katherine Beckett and Steve Herbert (2009, p. 20) explain, the refusal of homeless persons to remain exiled from prime spaces

> reveals a mismatch between official understandings of problem areas and how the banished experience those same places. Officials tend to imagine these neighbourhoods almost exclusively in terms of the degree to which they house and tempt the deviant. The banished, on the other hand, offer rich accounts of the historical and symbolic significance of those same areas, as well as the importance of the social networks and services they contain.

Given these strong attachments, it is unsurprising that efforts to confine the homeless to marginalized spaces failed and cyclical patterns of return to, or circulation within, prime spaces occurred.

Joseph best demonstrated the strong attachments homeless persons often have to prime spaces and the futility of police efforts to displace the homeless to marginalized spaces. Despite fines and incarceration, he exhibited a relentless resolve to return to the streets he considers his home:

> They [the police] tell me, "Get off [Whyte] Ave." I will be like, "You guys can go ahead and give me fines, you can go ahead and arrest me, put me in jail for unpaid fines, for warrants, but you guys know what, I

am going to come back to the Ave. It doesn't matter if I am in jail for 10 days, 20 days, or whatever. You guys are going to see me on the Ave either way… I am not going to leave the Ave. I am not. I don't care what you guys do, I am not leaving. I am sorry I can't do it. I choose not to do it."

Joseph's refusal to leave reflected the strong ties he had to Whyte Avenue. Over the years he claimed and defended particular locations as his spots for requesting help and so understandably saw the area as home. He seldom voluntarily left "the Ave."

Jail, fines, and move-outs do not deter marginalized persons like Joseph who imbue prime spaces with a sense of home. These spaces are among the few locales providing enough predictability and safety to ensure the street-involved meet their day to day needs. All participants refused to be permanently removed from these prime spaces. Regardless of what was done to them they wanted and needed to be in the prime spaces they called home.

The Politics of Homeless Mobility

The constant movement of homeless persons between prime and marginalized spaces or within prime spaces reveals, as Blomley (2007, 2011, 2012) argues, that mobility is the enforced preference in public spaces (see also Feldman, 2004). Even the name for the privileged party in the begging encounter – "the passerby" – designates that movement is the preferred norm. Participants' stories extend Blomley's analysis, however, by discussing how this mobility occurs and the shape it takes. In particular, their strong ties to familiar prime spaces in which they meet their needs, the temporal limits of incarceration and police move-outs, and a continual impulsion to move-along so as to blend-in to busy prime spaces, lead to patterns of continual return to, and/or circular movement within, prime spaces. Moreover, as I will show below, participants' stories cast light on the politics of this constant mobility by revealing the negative and uneven consequences of these mobility patterns and by exposing that police agents are especially keen to problematize the stasis of homeless persons.

Participants clearly demonstrated that mobility was not good in and of itself nor was it simply an indication of privilege and power. Rather, they revealed that mobility could reflect disadvantage and have negative consequences. Specifically, although the homeless experience near constant movement, this relatively high mobility reflects attempts to make them less visible aspects of prime spaces. While it is tempting to see movement as freedom and so an indication of power (e.g., Razack, 2002a, 2002b), such constructions overlook the reasons for, and effects of, specific mobilities (Cresswell, 2012; Jocoy & Del Casino, 2010).

Participants wanted to stay in prime spaces and did not want to endure continual expulsion or constant movement in order to remain in the vicinity of their homes and workplaces. Their mobility patterns were not entirely of their own making. Rather, these movements stemmed from the exclusions brought about by the policing of homelessness. There would be no circulating in and out of jail, no need to return from the inner-city to prime space, and no need to move-along in order to blend into prime consumer spaces, if there were not efforts to eject the homeless from prime spaces in the first place. As Jocoy and Del Casino (2010, p. 157) remark, homeless persons' mobility patterns in city spaces reflect "powerlessness" and "the *space exclusion* ... that forces homeless people to be mobile." The mobility of homeless persons should thus not been equated to power, nor should it be constructed as apolitical (cf. Blomley, 2011, 2012; Razack, 2002b). Rather, a politics that aims to exclude the visibly homeless from certain spaces in order to fashion particular city spaces as prime or marginalized shapes the constant mobility of the homeless.

The consequences of these mobility patterns also challenge Blomley's (2007, 2011, 2012) suggestion that enforced mobility in public spaces is egalitarian and affects all persons in equal measure. Some participants experienced negative health repercussions from continual demands to move. Jason, for example, explained how constant demands to move-along led to exhaustion and truncated his ability to fulfill his basic human need for rest.

> Like I stay up for three days, sleep maybe for a day, and then am up the next day for three days again. I finally collapsed on the bench there, uh, somewhere down Whyte [Avenue] here. And I must have just dozed off. About fifteen minutes later, shake, shake, shake. Here is this cop standing over me. He says, "What are you doing here?" I looked at him and said, "I am trying to sleep." He said, "Unfortunately you are not allowed. People are not allowed to sleep on these things." And I go, "Ok. Uh, I am gone." Three days later, on another place I thought would be safe to sleep in a back alley, a nice little quite place. I put some cardboard there, laid down, put some cardboard over top on me. The same guy showed up and his partner.

Jason is constantly told to move-along and so will "stay up for three days" at a time until he "collapses." He explained that he "has got insomnia like you wouldn't believe." There is nowhere for him to rest within prime spaces, yet, like most other participants, rather than utilize shelter beds within dangerous marginalized inner-city spaces, Jason just keeps moving and so faces utter exhaustion. Overtiredness was common among participants. When asked where they stayed the night before, some participants answered that they had been up all night. Rick, for example, declared, "Actually, you know, last night I didn't sleep at all. I have been up 24 hours."

Other participants coped with the demands to keep moving through drugs or alcohol. Marie, for instance, explained that constant demands to move-along exacerbated her crack addiction.

> It is too hard to fall asleep. ... You fall asleep and you got people kicking you out of places. It is impossible to do it [sleep]. Like me right now, it [crack] just keeps me going. I don't even do it for the fucking high anymore; I think it is more that it just keeps me going. Because I don't want to fall asleep somewhere because I am scared of getting stopped by a police officer or security is going to wake me up and tell me to leave. Or I am going to get in shit. Or I am going to get banned from a place. So it just keeps me going right now.

Marie's discussion of how crack just "keeps [her] going" shows that these mobility patterns can carry serious negative consequences.

The enforced mobility brought about by policing efforts thus jeopardizes the health of the homeless by making them sleep-deprived or encouraging their addictions. These unhealthy lifestyles, in turn, make it more difficult to secure housing (National Coalition for the Homeless, 2009; Tanner, 2009). When policing constitutes mobility as the primary function of public spaces, people like Jason, Rick, and Marie who live their entire days in these spaces face greater exposure to the negative consequences of constant motion.

Businesses' Interests

Participants' stories further revealed the uneven burden of constant movement by showing that police agents did not demand mobility of all persons in public space. Rather, the enforced mobility of prime consumer spaces unfolds in unequal ways that allow obvious consumers to remain stationary. For instance, redevelopment plans commonly eliminate or reduce places, like comfortable benches, on which persons could relax (Hayward, 2004). Instead businesses provide most of the comfortable places for rest in prime spaces. However, people can rest in malls, bars, restaurants, or line-ups only if they purchase goods or services or are likely to do so. Money, which homeless persons do not have and cannot make without facing police action, mediates access to these facilities of rest.

Many participants described how whenever they accessed these public spaces of consumption for rest, policing agents quickly identified them as non-consumers, accused them of disorderly behaviour like panhandling, and told them to move-along. For instance, none of the visibly homeless who called Downtown home reported that they could go into the neighbourhood's main shopping mall. Darlene explained that security banned her from the mall on the false grounds that she was panhandling customers:

> Yeah. They [security] ban a lot of us. … I was actually attacked by one, and I defended myself, and two others came along. They roughed me up and brought me into a holding cell. … They said I was panhandling. … They roughed me up and I am barred from there.

Rick described a more typical scenario facing visibly homeless persons accessing the same mall. He said, "Yeah, they [security] told me that you are not allowed in here anymore period. … I was just hanging out. … It was open. It was daytime hours." Security banned Rick, like many other visibly homeless persons, from this allegedly public space despite the fact that he was not doing anything disruptive.

Police agents thus exclude the street-involved, like Rick and Darlene, from accessing this potential space of rest. Despite the fact that the mall is open to the public, Rick is kicked out for "hanging out" while obviously not consuming. Similarly, Darlene's appearance as a homeless person and not an ideal consumer gets her quickly accused of panhandling and violently banned from the mall. Businesses benefit from this policing insofar as they get a near-monopoly on places of rest. Moreover, because rest becomes a commodity businesses can ensure that homeless persons, who cannot access this commodity, are not static and highly visible features of prime spaces.

If we look at policing outside of businesses and on the sidewalk it is also clear that police agents do not uniformly demand mobility of all persons. This is particularly obvious when police officers and security guards chase away homeless persons from stationary and obstructive groups of consumers who block the sidewalk but are waiting in line to get into restaurants and bars. Participants who lived along Jasper Avenue and Whyte Avenue, spots with thriving night-time economies, illustrated that police agents did not allow them to solicit money from persons in the lineups outside bars. Joseph, for example, explained, "Like yeah sure I will ask people in front of the bars for money and stuff," but bouncers only allow him to stay a short while before they tell him, "Yo Joe you got to go, you been here a little bit." Although the clients from whom Joseph is requesting aid are not moving and are impeding traffic flow, Joe, the homeless man, is the only person who cannot remain in the space. In instances where he has refused to move-along, he has quickly faced abuse from bouncers or fines from police officers.

Dan also confirmed that police agents are nice to him only if he keeps moving. When asked how bouncers treat him, he stated, "They are pretty good. As long as you are not sitting there panhandling in front of the door where they are standing, if you are walking by or something." Police agents are there only to ensure that he keeps moving and "walking by." They are not enforcing movement among the consumers blocking sidewalks.

The fact that consumers can access public spaces of rest or remain immobile in public space while homeless persons cannot suggests that the policing of mobility does not unfold in egalitarian and apolitical ways as Blomley (2007, 2011, 2012) suggests. Blomley correctly observes there are bylaws about the location of businesses and their implements or customers, but either these bylaws permit consumers to be immobile or police agents are less concerned with enforcing these bylaws. In contrast, homeless persons are not allowed to be static features of prime spaces at any time. The homeless cannot access the businesses in which they might get a break from mobility, nor do they have their own private spaces which would guarantee moments of rest. Blomley's (2011, p. 32) suggestion that a police logic of pedestrian enforces mobility in ways such that a "yuppie and a beggar are placed on the same evaluative plane" might ring true among the discourses used to support anti-panhandling laws, but it does not reflect the policed lives of the homeless on the sidewalk.

Mobility Perpetuates the Policing of Homelessness

Businesses, however, are not the only parties who find their interests advanced by the constant mobility of the homeless. The circulatory patterns of mobility and the temporal repetition they contain also perpetuate the policing of homelessness and so advance the interest of police agents. Police agents arguably employ move-alongs or move-outs because such displacements provide pragmatic and easy solutions to demands from powerful business agents to rid prime spaces of homeless persons (Beckett & Herbert, 2009; Comack, 2012; King & Dunn, 2004). Moving the street-involved into marginalized spaces demonstrates that the police are doing something to appease the business actors who constitute the visibly homeless as a problem. It is easier to displace the homeless to the jail or the inner-city than it is to solve homelessness (Beckett & Herbert, 2009; King & Dunn, 2004). Moreover, some officers might genuinely believe that their actions are more compassionate and helpful to the homeless compared to other legal responses at their disposal (Pierce, 2010, n.p.). Nonetheless, the limited temporality of these displacements benefits police officers and security guards because the inevitable failure to contain the homeless in marginalized spaces reinforces the need for policing. Among participants, Steve and Marie best demonstrated how circulatory mobility and temporary displacement perpetuate and legitimate the policing of homelessness. Homeless persons in need must go to where the affluent congregate to request help. Steve revealed how the inevitable return of homeless persons to prime spaces gave some police agents excitement and job stability. He explained the joy of one security guard who continually chased his girlfriend, Marie, away from a Downtown strip mall:

> Buddy [the security guard] gets off on it. I talk to him all the time. ... We had been gone for like 6 months and I come down here one day looking for her. And he [the security guard] goes, "Oh I miss you guys. I miss the action." He liked that. I said, "That is kind of twisted." And he goes, "Well a little bit, but it is so boring around here. I miss your girlfriend chasing her back and forth."

Steve perceptively noted the "twisted" nature of these circulatory mobility patterns. Without a continual return of Marie to the site, the security guard's workday is "boring" and uneventful. Marie's misfortune and poverty are the security guard's excitement as every time she returns to seek aid she also re-injects "action" into his job.

Without homeless persons like Marie it is not clear that this security officer would have much to do. It is well-recognized that many spatially-underpinned policing methods tend to simply displace heavily-policed populations and so eventually lead to additional calls for police responses (Hogeveen & Freistadt, 2012). In the case of homeless persons, the return of most homeless persons to prime spaces frustrates many police agents (King & Dunn, 2004), yet it simultaneously ensures that they have a continual supply of work. By constantly "chasing" the homeless "back and forth" or by repeatedly placing them in and out of jail, police agents only temporarily displace the homeless and so are continually called upon to address the presence of homeless persons in prime spaces.

Racialized Homeless Mobility Patterns

Although policing created continual movement among all homeless persons, the specific patterns of mobility differed among participants. Just as marginalized spaces were racialized, so too were the mobility patterns of the homeless. Because, as the previous chapter showed, Aboriginal homeless persons were more readily ushered into the jail or the inner-city, they more frequently engaged in circular patterns of mobility that entailed moving from these distant marginalized spaces back to prime spaces. As such, they bore more of the dangers associated with displacement to these marginalized spaces and had to travel greater distances to return to their homes. Meanwhile, White homeless persons' mobility patterns consisted predominately of circulation within prime spaces. In fact, all the stories about move-alongs initiated by EPS officers involved White homeless persons. Security guards demanded all homeless persons, regardless of racial identity, move-along, but police officers, who unlike security guards had the ability to escort homeless persons out of areas, only moved-along White homeless persons. None of the Aboriginal participants discussed encounters with police officers that permitted them to remain in prime consumer spaces. Rather, if they came in contact with police officers, they were fined or moved-out to the McCauley-Boyle inner-city.

Police practices that force homeless Aboriginals to circulate between prime and marginalized spaces more thoroughly remove these persons from prime spaces and so reinforce the idea that prime spaces are ideally White spaces. Racialized mobility patterns that are more likely to send Aboriginal homeless persons to marginalized spaces ensure that they are less likely to be features of prime spaces, whether static or mobile. Because their movements send them further away, homeless Aboriginal persons have less opportunity to generate complaints in prime consumer spaces. As such, the mobility patterns of homeless Aboriginals grant policing agents more time where they do not have to deal with demands to ensure prime spaces like Old Strathcona and Downtown remain whitewashed and free of visibly homeless Aboriginal persons.

Moreover, the dangers involved in mobility patterns between prime and marginalized spaces are greater than the dangers found in circulating within prime spaces. Having to move through marginalized spaces means more exposure to the crime and violence characteristic of these spaces and less of the protection and security established within prime spaces. William King and Thomas Dunn (2004) argue that the dangerous conditions of some police displacements are likely meant to further dissuade persons from returning. When police move-outs force homeless Aboriginal persons into more dangerous mobility patterns, Aboriginal persons are more thoroughly eliminated from prime consumer spaces. For instance, Debrah, an Aboriginal homeless woman who calls Old Strathcona home, explained that returning to the area from the McCauley-Boyle inner-city involves a cold, "long," and "dangerous" "walk across the bridge" over the North Saskatchewan River. This particular mobility pattern not only ensures that she is not seen in Old Strathcona for the duration of her "long" walk, the dangers associated with this walk, which police officers might not be fully aware of, increase the possibility that something drastic will happen to her along the way and so she will not be able to return the prime space she calls home.

The constant mobility the policing of homelessness produces arguably reinforces longstanding stereotypes that homeless people (Cresswell, 2011; Hannam, Sheller & Urry, 2006; Jocoy & Del Casino, 2010) and Aboriginals (Goldberg, 1993) are nomadic and therefore do not have legitimate claims to prime spaces. Popular discourse often depicts the homeless as "tramps" without settled places to call home (Cresswell, 2011). Some commentators, like Paul Letkemann (2004, p. 243), have further suggested that homelessness attracts Aboriginal persons because it reflects the traditional practices of nomadism among "hunter-gathers." Such claims, however, overlook the external forces that create these mobility patterns and the colonial context in which this mobility unfolds (Peters, 2012). The racialized mobility patterns policing produces among the homeless ought to be viewed in this context, which Renisa Mawani and David Sealy (2011) observe continues in the present in mutated ways.

Indeed, the parallels between the contemporary racialized policing of homelessness and older colonial controls are striking. Colonial administrators used claims that Aboriginal persons were nomadic, and that nomadism was inferior, to support arguments that White settlers could claim lands as their own because there were apparently no settled inhabitants (Goldberg, 1993; Mawani, 2005; Razack, 2002b). Colonial states then set aside lands for Aboriginal settlement through the reserve system and dissolved Aboriginal rights to prime spaces so that Europeans could claim these lands. Meanwhile, Aboriginal access to these prime White spaces was guarded by Indian Agents and the pass system (Goldberg, 1993; Lawrence, 2002; Mawani, 2005; Peters & Robillard, 2009; Razack, 2002a, 2002b; Samuelson & Monture-Angus, 2002). Similarly, the contemporary policing of homelessness attempts to force disadvantaged Aboriginal persons into marginalized spaces and denies them full access to prime spaces. When homeless Aboriginals refuse to remain in marginalized spaces, police agents quickly send them back and/or set them in motion such that they cannot achieve a sense of permanent home and belonging within spaces set aside for consumer capitalism and White persons. This enforced mobility continues to depict marginalized Aboriginal persons as nomadic and in so doing overlooks how homeless Aboriginal persons often have settled roots, hold ideas of particular spaces as home, and have pre-existing claims to prime White spaces like Old Strathcona and Downtown. Constantly enforcing mobility among Aboriginal homeless persons in prime spaces ensures that if they want to settle in city spaces, they can do so only in the marginalized inner-city spaces reserved for them. Policing and enforced mobility thus intersect with race in ways that re-affirm old colonial spatial controls and protect White domination over prime spaces.

Conclusion: Transformative Spaces Must Be Spaces in Which All Persons Can Settle

Participants' stories demonstrate that they are not simply shunted and confined to marginalized spaces but that they experience patterns of near-constant mobility that serve the interests of businesses, perpetuate policing, and reinforce racial hierarchies. Scholars who advance the civic sanitation argument focus predominately on gentrifying spaces and so do not look at movement between city spaces (Hannam, Sheller & Urry, 2006). Blomley (2007, 2011, 2012) contends that an egalitarian and apolitical police logic of pedestrianism underpins anti-homeless ordinances, but his focus does not illuminate how the mobility underpinning this logic plays out on the street and in the lives of the homeless. Meanwhile, discussions of the policing and the racialization of space, such as Razack's (2002a, 2002b), argue that policing confines Aboriginal persons to marginalized spaces and so reduces their mobility. These positions, however, do not consider what persons do once shunted to marginalized spaces nor do they fully recognize how mobility can produce or reflect both privilege and disadvantage. Inspired by scholarship from the "mobilities turn" in the social sciences (Hannam, Sheller & Urry, 2006), particularly Cresswell's (2006, 2010, 2012) demand to sketch the "politics of mobility" by looking at lived experience, I have detailed how certain actors benefit from a policing that makes homeless persons continually return from marginalized spaces to prime spaces or constantly move-along within prime spaces.

The mobility brought about by the policing of homelessness and urban space reinforces the exclusion of the homeless. The street-involved, especially Aboriginal homeless persons, apparently belong only in marginalized spaces and when they refuse to remain there they find themselves caught in mobility patterns that deny their sense of home and jeopardize their health and safety. Constant movement between prime and marginalized spaces, or continual motion within prime spaces, are harmful and dehumanizing. These mobility patterns buy police agents time where they temporarily do not have to deal with demands to remove homeless persons from prime spaces. This enforced mobility also helps constitute prime spaces as zones of consumption by demanding circulation, commodifying rest, and decreasing the visibility of homelessness. Moreover, these mobilities are racialized in ways that affirm prime spaces as White spaces while attempting to prevent street-involved Aboriginal persons from settling in spaces outside marginalized inner-city neighbourhoods.

Highlighting how the policing of homelessness produces mobility in the interests of some and not others undercuts claims that the logic underpinning anti-homeless ordinances and municipal policing is apolitical or egalitarian. Demonstrating these politics is a first step to challenging these laws and policing practices. Moreover, recognizing that mobility does not benefit everyone and is not always something to celebrate whenever it manifest in public spaces holds significant implications for efforts to create new and inclusive public spaces. The mobility patterns produced by the policing of homelessness help ensure that housed persons who utilize prime spaces do not encounter static and visibly homeless persons for any meaningful duration. Enforcing constant mobility among the homeless therefore has the same effect as confining the marginalized into areas where they are out of sight – it truncates the ability of prime public spaces to become political platforms by removing the visibly poor and racial minorities from public consciousness (Martin, 2002; Mosher, 2002).

The more fleeting the contact between strangers in public spaces is, the less likely public spaces can turn into arenas were marginalized persons can demonstrate inequality and the attendant need for social action. Social change, as Don Mitchell (2004) convincingly argues, requires a motivated public that takes space – lives in it, occupies it. A true political public sphere cannot be something that persons simply pass through. It cannot be something that unquestioningly glorifies mobility. Rather, a public sphere with transformative potential must be something all persons, regardless of their race, can inhabit, settle within, and call home.

CONCLUSION

HEEDING THE VOICES OF THE HOMELESS AND POLICED: SUMMARY, IMPLICATIONS, AND FUTURE DIRECTIONS

Increased homelessness has led many cities to develop policing responses, such as anti-homeless ordinances, that attempt to remove homeless persons from public spaces (see for e.g., Collins & Blomley, 2003; Hermer & Mosher, 2002; Mitchell, 2004; Feldman, 2004). Those who have created, enforced, or researched these measures have largely overlooked the experiences of the homeless who are subject to subject these efforts. Consequently, although increases in homelessness reflect economic shifts and policy changes (Beckett & Herbert, 2009; Hulchanski, Campsie, Chau, Hwang & Paradis, 2009; Jordan, 1999; Lenon, 2000; Lyon-Callo, 2000; O'Grady, Gaetz & Buccieri, 2011; Rahimian, Wolch & Koegel, 1992), policing efforts to address this problem continue unabated. Edmonton, for instance, has recently joined other major urban centres' policing efforts by developing an anti-panhandling bylaw and a diverted giving campaign. This book has used Edmonton as backdrop in order to examine the experiences of homeless persons subject to these and other policing efforts. It asked: How do the homeless experience policing?

I used this question and 22 in-situ interviews with homeless adults to assess existing arguments in the literature on the policing of homelessness and to help resolve debates among these arguments concerning what the policing of homelessness does, the politics behind this policing, and how to respond to this policing. Following William Miller & Benjamin Crabtree (2004), interviews tapped the experiences of homeless persons by capturing stories about their everyday lives. I have argued that the stories of the homeless reveal that Edmonton's new anti-panhandling efforts hold problematic assumptions about street life and contribute to a racialized policing of homelessness, space, and mobility. This concluding chapter reflects on the implications of my argument and findings. First, I review how this research has extended existing literature. Second, I discuss the suggestions my findings make for responding to homelessness and the policing thereof. I close by documenting the areas of future research this study highlights.

Contributions to Previous Literature and Debates

While previous literature has focused predominately on the language and development of anti-homeless ordinances (e.g., Gordon, 2006; Hermer & Mosher, 2002; Mitchell, 2004), the stories of the homeless demonstrate the utility of expanded conceptions of policing, such as Mark Neocleous' (2000), that connect officers and the laws they discretionarily apply to the broader realms of social policy, social work, and social service provision. To be sure, police officers' enforcement of the law played an important role in the everyday lives of the homeless, but so too did their informal responses such as move-outs and move-alongs. Moreover, the actions and claims of security guards, charitable agencies, policy makers, urban planners, and diverted giving campaign officials helped shape the lives of the homeless. Specifically, this book has shown how urban planning policies and the HHGS campaign justified and worked alongside police agents' formal and informal responses in order to reduce visible homelessness in prime consumer spaces. By paying attention to all these responses and actors I have provided a fuller understanding of the policing of homelessness and the experience thereof.

Previous research concerning the policing of homeless falls into four major arguments: the broken windows theory (Wilson & Kelling, 1982), the production of the proletariat argument (Gordon, 2006, 2010), the civic sanitation argument (e.g., Feldman, 2004; Mitchell, 2004; Mosher, 2002; O'Grady, Gaetz & Buccieri, 2011), and the pedestrianism position (Blomley, 2007, 2011, 2012). Each of these arguments holds a different position on what the policing of homelessness (justifiably or not) accomplishes. As such, each argument holds different views about the politics, if any, behind the policing of homelessness and what, if anything, ought to be done to address this policing. Few of these scholars, however, consider how these policing efforts unfold in practice and affect the lives of homeless persons. Moreover, because previous research does not pay attention to the individuals these policing efforts target, it has overlooked how the policing of homelessness creates and reinforces differences based on racial identity.

By collecting and analyzing the stories of homeless persons I have examined how the policing of homelessness unfolds on the ground, whose interest it protects, and how it is racialized. In so doing I have considered the extent to which the experiences of the homeless reflect the claims behind the four major positions. I have also demonstrated that there is, in fact, a politics behind the policing of homelessness that cannot be fully understood without examining how that policing is racialized. These interventions required integrating into existing arguments conceptions of "prime and marginalized spaces" (Feldman, 2004; Wardhaugh, 1996; Wardhaugh & Jones, 1999), ideas about the "politics of mobility" (Cresswell, 2006, 2010, 2012), and research on racialized space and policing (Comack, 2012, Goldberg, 1993; Razack, 2002a, 2002b; Mawani, 2002, 2012).

My research has challenged the broken windows theory. I have discussed the links between broken windows theorists and the claims of those who have supported Edmonton's anti-panhandling efforts, such as EPS authorities, HHGS officials, and business leaders. These persons argue that anti-panhandling efforts target the aggressive behaviour of individuals who incite fear among passersby. As such, they contend that anti-homeless ordinances work for the common good because they prevent crime and ensure order (e.g., Elanik, 2009; Kelling & Coles, 1997; Wilson & Kelling, 1982). They further argue that measures that push the homeless into charities, like diverted giving campaigns or informal police move-outs, encourage public safety while ensuring that panhandlers receive the services they need (e.g., City of Edmonton, 2010b; Kelling & Coles, 1997; Pierce, 2010, n.p.). This book, however, has demonstrated that Edmonton's anti-panhandling efforts are used to draw police attention to all visibly homeless persons, not just (aggressive) panhandlers. I have also shown that ostensibly benevolent attempts to expel the homeless into charities ignore how the level of services among these agencies, and the fashion in which these services are delivered, do not align with the lives and preferences of the entire street-involved population. Additionally, I have argued that attempts to justify anti-panhandling efforts by depicting the homeless as frauds, criminals, addicts, and/or intimidators are exaggerated and decontextualized.

Anti-panhandling supporters and broken windows theorists thus make several problematic assumptions about street life. These assumptions justify the policing of homelessness while keeping many homeless persons tied to the streets. While broken windows theorists and others who support anti-homeless ordinances and diverted giving campaigns argue that these measures prevent crime and should be expanded, this research has echoed that of William O'Grady, Stephen Gaetz, and Kristy Buccieri (2011) and demonstrated that these policing efforts unfairly target the visibly homeless, do little to help the street-involved, and so ought to be eliminated.

I have also challenged the production of the proletariat argument advanced by Todd Gordon (2006, 2010). Gordon's work contends that anti-homeless ordinances such as Edmonton's revised Public Places Bylaw (2009) resurrect vagrancy laws and protect capital interests by forcing those who refuse wage labour into precarious employment. In contrast, this study has shown that the policing of homelessness targets the visibly homeless regardless of their relations to wage labour. Standing out in consumer spaces attracts police attention, not employment status. Gordon correctly emphasizes that policing operates in the interests of capital, but those interests are protected by removing visible homelessness from prime consumer spaces and not by forcing the homeless to become members of the proletariat. In fact, several participants' stories demonstrated that they were already tied to the precarious work Gordon says the policing of homelessness promotes, yet they were still policed because of their appearance in consumer spaces. Meanwhile, visibly homeless persons drew less police attention when they blended into marginalized spaces and individuals who were homeless but looked like consumers dodged police attention in prime spaces.

My demonstration of the appearance-based and spatially-underpinned policing of homelessness aligns with the civic sanitation argument's claim that anti-homeless efforts aim to cleanse public spaces of visible homelessness in order to help attract investment and consumers (e.g., Berti & Sommers, 2010; Feldman, 2004; O'Grady, Gaetz & Buccieri, 2011; Mitchell, 2004). The stories of the homeless, however, extend this position. In particular, I have shown how homeless persons are not simply expelled from prime consumer spaces, but are displaced to the dangerous marginalized spaces of the jail and the inner-city through fines and move-outs. Moreover, I have demonstrated that the use of fines and move-outs was racialized. These racialized police practices, coupled with long-standing discrimination against Aboriginal peoples in the criminal justice system and urban planning policies, helped constitute marginalized spaces as spaces of Aboriginality while protecting the idea that prime spaces are White spaces. As such, this research has revealed how the racialized policing of space documented by scholars like Sherene Razack (2002a, 2002b), Elizabeth Comack (2012), and Renisa Mawani (2002, 2012) plays out in the policing of homelessness.

I have also advanced this literature on the racialized policing of space by demonstrating that homeless persons did not remain confined to marginalized spaces. Rather, homeless persons continued to be tied to the prime spaces that they considered their home. These ties meant that the policing of homeless created constant mobility patterns among the homeless. Those homeless individuals that police officers moved to marginalized spaces, which consisted overwhelmingly of Aboriginal persons, continually circulated between the marginalized spaces they were shunted to and the prime spaces from which they were removed. In other cases, homeless persons engaged in constant circulation within prime spaces because police agents frequently told them to move-along or because they wished to avoid contact with police agents in the first place.

By documenting the mobility patterns of the homeless this book affirms the importance Nikolas Blomley (2007, 2011, 2012) gives to mobility in his pedestrianism position. However, whereas Blomley concludes that municipal laws about public space manifest an apolitical police logic of pedestrianism that glorifies mobility, I have demonstrated how the policing inspired by anti-homeless efforts like Edmonton's revised Public Places Bylaw (2009) shapes the mobility of homeless persons and unfolds in the interests of powerful agents. I have thus argued that that there is a politics behind the policing of homelessness. The stories of homeless persons demonstrate that their immobility is a higher priority to police agents than the stasis of consumers. Moreover, forcing the homeless into constant motion protects business interests by commodifying rest and temporarily removing visible signs of poverty from consumer spaces. Meanwhile, the nearly-inevitable return of homeless persons to prime spaces perpetuates the policing of homelessness and so advances the interests of police agents. The racialization of displacement further means the mobility patterns of the homeless are also racialized. Aboriginal persons have to endure longer and more dangerous movements as they frequently circulate between prime and marginalized spaces. This racialized mobility helps constitute prime spaces as White spaces because it ensures that homeless Aboriginal persons cannot settle in these spaces. I have thus contended that the policing of homelessness reflects older colonial controls that assumed Aboriginal people were nomadic, tried to confine them to marginalized spaces, and denied claims they already had to prime spaces.

My overarching argument that Edmonton's anti-panhandling efforts hold problematic assumptions about street life and contribute to a racialized policing of homelessness, space, and mobility thus rejects the broken windows theory and the claims of those who supported Edmonton's new policing initiatives, challenges the production of the proletariat argument, and refines both the civic sanitation argument and the pedestrianism position. While these arguments hold different positions on what the policing of homelessness does, participants' stories have shown that this policing, as it unfolds on the ground in myriad ways, attempts to remove the visibly homeless from prime spaces and in so doing creates racialized spaces and patterns of mobility.

The four different arguments among the previous literature also hold varying positions on the parties, if any, that have their interests protected by the policing of homelessness. I have argued that by temporarily displacing the visibly homeless from prime spaces and trying to shunt homeless Aboriginals into marginalized spaces the interests of businesses and police agents are protected while racial hierarchies are maintained. Documenting this politics has challenged claims that the policing of homelessness is apolitical insofar as it protects the interests of the common good by preventing crime (Wilson & Kelling, 1982; Kelling & Coles, 1997) or by ensuring the free mobility of everyone (Blomley, 2011, 2012). Moreover, I have extended the claims of the production of the proletariat argument (Gordon, 2006, 2010) and the civic sanitation argument (e.g., Berti & Sommers, 2010; Feldman, 2004; Mitchell, 2004; O'Grady, Gaetz and Buccieri, 2011) by clarifying how the policing of homelessness protects the interests of business owners and by showing that other parties also benefit from this policing.

Creating Inclusive Spaces: Suggestions for Responding to Homelessness and the Policing Thereof

This book has sympathized with the civic sanitation argument's position that expelling the homeless from public space reduces encounters with the poor and so curtails the ability for collective action on the topic of homelessness (Feldman, 2004; Martin, 2002; Mosher, 2002; Mitchell, 1997, 2004). Although I have shown that this expulsion is neither total nor uniform, I have argued that the near-constant mobility that the policing of homelessness ensures continues to deny the homeless, especially Aboriginal homeless persons, any chances to settle in prime space and so still truncates the ability of these spaces to become platforms for transformative action. Thus, while I have echoed the civic sanitation argument's call to create inclusive city spaces (Feldman, 2004; Mitchell, 1997, 2004; Mitchell & Heynen, 2009; Mosher, 2002), my findings have highlighted several important things to consider when trying to redress the policing of homelessness in order to create more diverse and welcoming city spaces.

For instance, I have shown that the homeless are policed through a variety of actors and practices. As such, my findings align with Blomley's (2011) assessment that legal challenges to anti-homeless ordinances are insufficient. To be sure, as Gordon (2006), Dianne Martin (2002), O'Grady, Gaetz, and Buccieri (2011), and Arthur Schaefer (2007) argue, efforts should be made to strike down laws like Edmonton's revised Public Places Bylaw (2009). Creating inclusive spaces, however, also requires attending to the other ways the homeless are policed and acknowledging the racialized nature of this policing.

In particular, participants' stories have shown that experiences of the policing of homelessness are shaped by spatial and racial divisions. Police agents contribute to these divisions by more readily ushering Aboriginal persons to marginalized spaces. As such, these police practices should be challenged. However, I have also documented how the racialized displacement that underpins the policing of homelessness reflects how the criminal justice system and the inner-city have already been fashioned into racialized and marginalized spaces. Consequently, challenges to the racialized policing of homelessness must echo critiques that highlight how the criminal justice system is inappropriately used to respond to social policy failures and to confine persons of non-White racial identity (e.g., Samuelson & Monture-Angus, 2002; Wacquant, 2009, 2012). Similarly, those who want to undercut the racialized policing of homelessness need to join arguments that admonish the concentration of poverty and persons of non-White racial identity in specific neighbourhoods (e.g., La Prairie, 2002; Wacquant, 2000, 2008). Diversity should be encouraged throughout the city (Feldman, 2004). Urban planners should not be continuing to concentrate affordable housing, social services, and explicitly Aboriginal spaces in the inner-city. Every neighbourhood ought to welcome of the poor, various social services, and all persons regardless of their racial identity.

Attempts to create diverse and inclusive spaces by spreading affordable housing programs, Aboriginal services, and charitable organizations throughout the city, however, must also consider the changes that need to occur within the social services agencies. My findings have revealed ways existing social services are unwelcoming because they do not align with the lived experiences and preferences of the entire street-involved population. I have outlined several recommendations that could make charitable organizations more inclusive spaces and could help ensure that their policing responses better reflected the desires of homeless persons. Moreover, I have argued that improving direct income assistance to the homeless could reduce reliance on these organizations and thereby curtail their mechanisms of policing while allowing homeless persons to achieve the autonomy and direct consumption they sought from the informal economy. Additionally, such income redistribution would begin to address the economic hardships that underpin homelessness in the first place (Hulchanski, Campsie, Chau, Hwang & Paradis, 2009). Ending homelessness is one way to curb the policing of homelessness. This research has shown, however, that efforts to do this will continue to be unsuccessful if they do not heed the voices of the homeless.

Creating venues for homeless persons' voices to be heard should therefore be of utmost priority to those interested in addressing homelessness and the policing thereof. Thus far public education campaigns, like Edmonton's HHGS campaign, have contributed to and justified the exclusion and policing of the homeless. As I have shown, these campaigns reflect the voices of business leaders and police officials while depicting a decontextualized and inaccurate image of panhandlers, homeless persons, and street life. In place of these voices and their one-sided messages, activists ought to develop public education efforts that project the voices and the experiences of the homeless. This study has provided an initial step in this direction by collecting and analyzing the stories of the homeless. A new public education campaign, however, could pay the homeless to tell their stories in the same way the HHGS campaign employs persons to visit prime spaces and spread its message. This would facilitate the encounters between the homeless and the housed that the civic sanitation argument contends are necessary to create inclusive city spaces (e.g., Martin, 2002; Mitchell, 2004). These encounters might produce greater understanding of homeless persons' experiences among passersby and so help create support for some of the program and policy changes listed throughout this chapter and this book.

Conclusion: Future Research Directions

My research thus highlights the many factors that those who wish to challenge the policing of homelessness must address, but future research will have to document the successful strategies people have used attend to these issues. What actions have been successful at striking down anti-homeless ordinances? Are there measures that can reduce the use of police move-outs and move-alongs? How can reliance on the criminal justice system as a response to social policy failure be reduced? How can the overrepresentation of Aboriginal peoples in the justice system be rectified? Have some communities resisted redevelopments that displace the homeless? How can cities ensure urban planning and new affordable housing developments do not create marginalized spaces in which poverty and persons of non-White racial identity are concentrated? How can social service providers ensure they heed the voices of the homeless? Is it possible to champion greater income redistribution in the contemporary political climate? How could activists create and implement an effective public education campaign that projects the stories of the homeless and compels individuals to welcome them in all public spaces? Are there examples of such homeless-led campaigns from which activists can learn? These are the challenging questions that researchers will have to continue to grapple with in order to push toward ameliorative change for the homeless.

The limits of this study point to several other productive areas of future research. The focus on Edmonton, for instance, leaves room for studies of other cities. Although the policing practices discussed by participants are increasingly common features of urban centres, local contexts will shape how each policing effort unfolds on the ground. Edmonton is unique because its proximity to eight adult correctional facilities contributes to the composition of its homeless population (Thomson, Knutson, deKoning, Grekul & Fawcett, 2010). It also has the second highest urban Aboriginal population in Canada (Environics Institute, 2010). This large Aboriginal population and the creation of the McCauley-Boyle area as the dominant social service region shape how the policing of homelessness is racialized in Edmonton. Marginalized and prime spaces do not naturally develop, nor are they simply the outcome of apolitical economic processes. Rather, the characteristics of these physical spaces are socially constructed through political decisions and struggles (Mitchell, 2004; Wacquant, 2008). Research on urban redevelopment shows that business leaders tend to dominate these struggles (Mitchell, 2004), but the specific spaces that will be set aside as marginalized or prime spaces will vary depending on the conduct of local actors. Additional case studies that investigate how the policing of homeless unfolds on the ground of other cities would help identify how these local struggles and contexts shape the policing of homelessness. Moreover, these studies might help identify ways certain cities have resisted policing initiatives and redevelopments that displace the marginalized.

My focus on how homeless persons experience policing underpins the contributions I make to this field, yet there are many other actors involved in the policing efforts that this book has engaged. Documenting the experiences of these other actors could offer additional perspectives on what the policing of homelessness does, how the politics behind it unfold, and how activists can counter the exclusion of homeless persons from public space. For example, efforts to police the homeless through diverted giving campaigns attempt to direct homeless persons off the street and into social services, but they also aim at the generosity of passersby (Hermer, 2001). It remains unclear how persons who offer direct aid to the homeless make sense of, experience, and resist these policing efforts. Investigating how these policing efforts shape housed persons' actions would help to fully illuminate the complex nature of these policing efforts. This research could also help identify allies of homeless persons and reveal additional strategies that might counter attempts to police and confine the homeless.

Additionally, examining a more diverse segment of the street-involved population could contribute to suggestions for improving responses to homelessness. This study's sample of participants comprised some of the most street-entrenched persons in Edmonton. I spoke with both absolutely and relatively homeless individuals who spent their daytime hours in prime consumer spaces and so were most likely to draw police attention while least likely to integrate into social services and housing programs. Many impoverished Edmontonians have secured housing, addictions treatment, and improved income assistance (Homeward Trust Edmonton, 2012). It is necessary to document the experiences of these individuals in order to determine the full extent to which they have broken negative ties with the streets and police agents. For those who have managed to fully integrate into housed lifestyles, it is pertinent to identify the circumstances and actions that helped them do so in order to consider if and how these conditions and responses could be transferred to the more street-entrenched.

My sample of participants also does not reflect the full complexity of racial identities among the homeless. Homelessness befalls persons of all backgrounds (Hulchanski, Campsie, Chau, Hwang & Paradis, 2009) and so there are many racial identities that are not accounted for in this study. Moreover, while participants happened to report distinct racial identities that aligned with the physical markers commonly used to categorize individuals as White or Aboriginal, there are many individuals who do not fit neatly into these divisions and there is heterogeneity among these categories (Levine-Rasky, 2002; Mawani, 2010). This book is the first of its kind to document how distinctions between Aboriginal and White homeless persons shape the policing of homelessness, but future research should build on this by determining how the diverse racial identities encompassed in a category like "Aboriginal" (such as Cree or Métis) influence the policing of homelessness, if at all.

Additionally, future research can build upon my work by demonstrating how other differences, like gender, intersect with the racialized policing of homelessness. Although at times I have drawn attention to how gender and Aboriginal racial identity compound, this book has focused on the different experiences of White and Aboriginal homeless persons because of the vast overrepresentation of Aboriginal people in Edmonton's homeless population (Sorensen, 2012) and because of the well-documented ways the policing of Aboriginal people has been racialized (Comack, 2012; Razack, 2002a, 2002b). My intent has been to illuminate a gap in the literatures on racialized policing and the policing of homelessness, not to suggest that other schemes of categorization are less important to how the homeless experience policing.

Future research could also build upon this book by examining a broader or more nuanced idea of space. I have significantly advanced the literature on the policing of homelessness by drawing attention to how homeless persons experience urban space and how they encounter and move between and within prime and marginalized spaces. Ethnographic research confirms this dualistic division of space into prime and marginalized spaces (Feldman, 2004; Wardhaugh, 1996, Wardhaugh & Jones, 1999). However, all the research that makes this dualistic division draws its conclusions from homeless persons within these spaces. This is in large part because these are the spaces in which homeless persons are most visible and so can be accessed for data. Nevertheless, it is possible that there is a contingent of less-visible hidden homeless persons who, because of the unique locations in which they live, have different experiences of space and policing. When researchers discover a way to access this hidden homeless population they will be in a better position to build upon understandings of how these individuals are policed.

A more immediately available course of action by which researchers could expand the notion of space I have developed would be to examine the policing of homelessness outside of the city setting. Homelessness is not simply an urban phenomenon. It unfolds in unique forms in rural communities (Cloke, Milbourne & Widdowfield, 2003) and on Reserves (Peters, 2012). There is, however, little research on how police agents respond to homelessness in these contexts. Moreover, many homeless persons' biographies, especially those of homeless Aboriginals, cut across urban, rural, and Reserve contexts (Peters, 2012; Peters & Robillard, 2009). Future research ought to examine the policing of Aboriginal homelessness across urban and reserve contexts. In particular, researchers should consider how policing contributes to well-documented movements between these two settings (Peters & Robillard, 2009), how these mobilities themselves become efforts to police homeless Aboriginals, and how to develop more effective responses to the housing issues of this mobile population.

REFERENCES

Amnesty International. (2009). *No more stolen sisters: The need for a comprehensive response to discrimination and violence against Indigenous women in Canada.* London: Amnesty International Publications.

Anderson, D. (2009, June 1). *Panhandling – Alternative methods and targeted education campaign.* Edmonton: Edmonton Community Services Department. Retrieved from: http://webdocs.edmonton.ca/ OcctopusDocs/Public/Complete/Reports/CS/CSAM/2009-06-22/2009CSW014.doc.

Anti-panhandling campaign launched in Edmonton. (2010, July 20). *CBC News Online.* Retrieved from: http://www.cbc.ca/news/ canada/edmonton/story/2010/07/20/edmonton-panhandler-campaign-have-heart-give-smart.html.

Armitage, A. (1993). Family and child welfare in First Nations Communities. In B. Warf (Ed.), *Rethinking child welfare in Canada,* (pp. 131-170). Toronto: McCelland & Stewart.

Ashforth, B., Sluss, D.M., & Harrison, S.H. (2007). Socialization in organizational contexts. In G.P. Hodgkinson & J.K. Ford (Eds.,) *International Review of Industrial and Organizational Psychology, Vol. 22,* (pp. 1-70). Sussex, England: Wiley.

Beckett, K., & Herbert, S. (2009). *Banished: The new social control in urban America.* Oxford: Oxford University Press.

Belanger, Y. D., Weasel Head, G., & Awosoga, O. (2012). *Assessing urban Aboriginal housing and homelessness in Canada.* Ottawa: National Association of Friendship Centres & The Office of the Federal Interlocutor for Métis and Non-Status Indians.

Berg, B. (2004). *Qualitative research methods for the social sciences* (5th ed.). Boston: Pearson.

Berti, M., & Sommers, J. (2010). "The streets belong to people that pay for them": The spatial regulation of street poverty in Vancouver, British Columbia. In D. Crocker & V. M. Johnson (Eds.), *Poverty, regulation & social justice: Readings on the criminalization of poverty*, (pp. 60-74). Halifax: Fernwood.

Blackburn, D. (2000). Why race is not a biological concept. In B. Lang (Ed.), *Race and racism in theory and practice*, (pp. 3-26). New York: Rowman & Littlefield Publishers Inc.

Blomley, N. (2012). 2011 Urban Geography Plenary Lecture – Coloured rabbits, dangerous trees, and public sitting: Sidewalks, police and the city. *Urban Geography*, 33 (7), 917-935.

Blomley, N. (2011). *Rights of passage: Sidewalks and the regulation of public flow*. New York: Routledge.

Blomley, N. (2007). How to turn a beggar into a bus stop: Law, traffic and the 'function of the place.' *Urban Studies*, 44(9), 1697-1712.

Bright, D. (1995). Loafers are not going to subsist upon public credulence: Vagrancy and the law in Calgary, 1900-1914. *Labour/Le Travail*, 36, 37-58.

Brooymans, H. (2010, January 24). Flames lit for 46 homeless who died on the streets last year. *Edmonton Journal*, p. A5.

Brooks C. (2002). Globalization and a new underclass of "disposable people." In B. Schissel & C. Brooks (Eds.), *Marginality and condemnation*, (pp. 273-288). Halifax: Fernwood.

Brown, D. (1995). Transcending dichotomies: The criminal justice network and a dialogue concerning prisoners and victims. *Current Issues in Criminal Justice*, 6, 143-147.

Canadian Charter of Rights and Freedoms, s. 15, Part I of the Constitution Act, 1982, being Schedule B to the Canada Act 1982 (U.K.). (1982, c.11).

Chambliss, W. (1964). A sociological analysis of the law of vagrancy. *Social Problems*, 12, 67-77.

Chard, G., Faulkner, T., & Chugg, A. (2009). Exploring occupation and its meaning among homeless men. *British Journal of Occupational Therapy*, 72(3), 116-124.

City of Edmonton. (2011). *Strathcona area redevelopment plan*. Edmonton: City of Edmonton.

City of Edmonton. (2010a). *Capital city downtown plan*. Edmonton: City of Edmonton.

City of Edmonton. (2010b). *"Have a Heart, Give Smart" – Leaflet*. Edmonton: City of Edmonton & Edmonton Police Service. Retrieved from: http://www.edmonton.ca/for_residents/Have_a_Heart_Give_Smart_1 eaflet.pdf.

City of Edmonton. (2005a). *Community profile: Boyle Street.* Edmonton: City of Edmonton.

City of Edmonton. (2005b). *Community Profile: Edmonton.* Edmonton: City of Edmonton.

City of Edmonton. (2005c). *Community Profile: McCauley.* Edmonton: City of Edmonton.

Cloke, P., Milbourne, P., & Widdowfield, R. (2003). The complex mobilities of homeless people in rural England. *Geoforum, 34,* 21-35.

Collins, D., & Blomley, N. (2003). Private needs and public space: Politics, poverty, and anti-panhandling by-laws in Canadian Cities. In Law Commission of Canada (Ed.), *New Perspectives on the Public-Private Divide,* (pp. 40-67). Vancouver: UBC Press.

Comack, E. (2012). *Racialized policing: Aboriginal people's encounters with the police.* Fernwood: Halifax.

Cormier, R. (2008, December 13). Frigid temperatures swell homeless shelters: Winter emergency program used for the first time this season. *Edmonton Journal,* p. B4.

Council to consider plan to stop aggressive panhandling. (2009, January 23). *CBC News Online.* Retrieved from: http://www.cbc.ca/news/canada/edmonton/story/2009/01/23/edm-aggressive-panhandling.html.

Cresswell, T. (2012). Mobilities II: Still. *Progress in Human Geography, 36*(5), 645-653.

Cresswell, T. (2011). The vagrant/vagabond: The curious career of a mobile subject. In T. Cresswell & P. Merriman (Eds.), *Geographies of mobilities: Practices, spaces, subjects,* (pp. 239-253). Burlington: Ashgate.

Cresswell, Tim. (2010). Mobilities I: Catching up. *Progress in Human Geography, 35*(4), 550-558.

Cresswell, T. (2006). The right to mobility: The production of mobility in the courtroom. *Antipode,* 735-754.

Cresswell, T., & Merriman, P. (2011). Introduction: Geographies of mobilities – practices, spaces, subjects. In T. Cresswell & P. Merriman (Eds.), *Geographies of mobilities: Practices, spaces, subjects,* (pp. 1-15). Burlington: Ashgate.

Darlene James Policy & Business Planning. (2007). *Harm reduction policy background paper.* Edmonton: Darlene James Policy & Business Planning & Alberta Alcohol and Drug Abuse Commission.

Dean, H., & Melrose, M. (1999). Easy pickings or hard profession? Begging as an economic activity. In Hartley Dean (Ed.), *Begging questions: Street-level economic activity and social policy failure,* (pp. 83-100). Bristol: The Policy Press.

DeVerteuil, G. (2003). Homeless mobility, institutional settings, and the new poverty management. *Environment and Planning A, 35,* 361-379.

Donzelot, J. (1979). *The policing of families*. London: Hutchinson & Co.

Drake, L. (2009, January 25). City's homeless 'die ugly deaths': Memorial service held in memory of 47 lives lost last year. *Edmonton Journal*, p. A5.

Dubber, M., & Valverde, M. (2006). Introduction: Perspectives on the power and science of police. In M. Dubber and M. Valverde (Eds.), *The New Police Science: The Police Power in Domestic and International Governance*, (pp. 1-16). Stanford: Stanford University Press.

Duneier, M. (2001). *Sidewalk*. New York: Ferrar, Straus and Giroux.

Echenberg, H. & Jensen, H. (2008). *Defining and enumerating homelessness in Canada*. Ottawa: Library of Parliament.

Edmonton police warn of con-man who poses as welder. (2011, July 14). *Edmonton Journal Online*. Retrieved from: http://www.edmontonjournal.com/news/Edmonton+police+warn+poses+welder/5102997/story.html?cid=megadrop_story.

Edmonton Social Planning Council. (2011). *Tracking the trends: Edmonton's increasing diversity*. Edmonton: Edmonton Social Planning Council.

Edmonton Social Planning Council. (2009). *We must do better: It's time to make Alberta poverty-free*. Edmonton: Edmonton Social Planning Council.

Edmonton Social Planning Council. (2009, April). 2009 Alberta budget analysis. *fAct* sheet. Edmonton: Edmonton Social Planning Council.

Edmonton Social Planning Council. (2007, May). Rental Housing in Edmonton. *fActivist*. Edmonton: Edmonton Social Planning Council.

Elanik, D. (2009). *Public safety concerns related to panhandling*. Edmonton: Edmonton Police Service. Retrieved from: http://webdocs.edmonton.ca/OcctopusDocs/Public/Complete/Reports/CC/CSAM/2009-02-04/2009PCS2006 Attach 1.doc.

Ellickson, R. (1996). Controlling chronic misconduct in city spaces: Of panhandlers, skid rows and public-space zoning. *The Yale Law Journal*, 105(5), 1165-1248.

Environics Institute. (2010). *Urban Aboriginal peoples study: Edmonton report*. Toronto: Environics Institute.

EPSVideoOnline (2011). Community crime update – Aggressive panhandling. Retrieved from: http://www.youtube.com/watch?v=FYc-CemC34E.

Evans, J. (2012) Supportive measures, enabling restraint: Governing homeless 'street drinkers' in Hamilton, Canada. *Social and Cultural Geography*, 13(2), 185-200.

Feldman, L. (2004). *Citizens without shelter: Homelessness, democracy, and political exclusion*. Ithaca: Cornell University Press.

Fereday, J., & Muir-Cochrane, E. (2006). Demonstrating rigor using thematic analysis: A hybrid approach of inductive and deductive coding and themes development. *International Journal of Qualitative Methods*, 5(1), 80-92.

Ferguson, A. (2007, June 23). "This is not something that can be fixed with a bylaw." *Edmonton Journal*, p. B1.

Ferrell, J. (2006). *Empire of scrounge.* New York: New York University Press.

Foote, C. (1956). Vagrancy-type law and its administration. *Pennsylvania Law Review.* 104(5), 603-650.

Forchuk, C., Montgomery, P., Berman, H., Ward-Griffin, C., Csiernik, R., ... Riesterer, P. (2010). Gaining ground, losing ground: The paradoxes of rural homelessness. *Canadian Journal of Nursing Research*, 42(2), 138-152.

Foucault, M. (1991). Governmentality. In G. Burchell, C. Gordon, & P. Miller (Eds.), *The Foucault effect: Studies in governmentality,* (pp. 87-104). Chicago: University of Chicago Press.

Foucault, M. (1980). *Power/Knowledge: Selected interviews and other writings, 1972-1977,* (C. Gordon, Ed., C. Gordon, L. Marshall, J. Mepham, & K. Soper, Trans.). New York: Pantheon Books.

Freistadt, J. (2011). Understanding others' experience: Phenomenology and/beyond violence [Special Issue]. *Journal of Theoretical and Philosophical Criminology*, 3, 1-42.

Freistadt, J. (2010). Navigating potentially conflicting political rationalities: Discursive strategies about "family" in Alberta's child welfare law. *Canadian Journal of Family Law*, 26, 219-267.

Gaetz, S. (2004). Safe streets for whom? Homeless youth, social exclusion, and criminal victimization. *Canadian Journal of Criminology and Criminal Justice*, 46(4), 423-455.

Gaetz, S., & O'Grady, B. (2002). Making money: Exploring the economy of young homeless workers. *Work, Employment & Society*, 16, 433-456.

Gaetz, S., Tarasuk, V., Dachner, N., & Kirkpatrick, S. (2006). "Managing" homeless youth in Toronto: Mismanaging food access and nutritional well-being. *Canadian Review of Social Policy*, 58, 43-61.

Glasbeek, A. (2010). Apprehensive wives and intimidated mothers: Women, fear of crime, and the criminalization of poverty in Toronto. In D. Crocker & V. M. Johnson (Eds.), *Poverty, regulation & social justice: Readings on the criminalization of poverty* 9pp. 123-138). Halifax: Fernwood.

Goldberg, T. (1993). *Racist culture: Philosophy and the politics of meaning.* Malden. Massachusetts: Blackwell.

Golub, A., Johnson, B.D., Taylor, A., & Eterno, J. (2003). Quality-of-life policing: Do offenders get the message? *Policing: An International Journal of Police Strategies & Management*, 26(4), 690 – 707.

Goodman, L., Fels, K., Glenn, C., & Benitez, J. (2011). *No safe place: Sexual assault in the lives of homeless women.* Harrisburg, PA: National Resource Center on Domestic Violence.

Gordon, T. (2010). Understanding the role of law-and-order policies in Canadian cities. In D. Crocker & V.M. Johnson (Eds.), *Poverty, regulation*

& social justice: Readings on the criminalization of poverty, (pp. 33-42). Halifax: Fernwood.

Gordon, T. (2006). *Cops, crime and capitalism: The law-and-order agenda in Canada*. Halifax: Fernwood Publishing.

Gowan, T. (2009). New hobos or neo-romantic fantasy? Urban ethnography beyond the neoliberal disconnect. *Qualitative Sociology*, 32(3), 231-257.

Gowan, T. (2002). The nexus: Homelessness and incarceration in two American cities. *Ethnography*, 3(4), 500-534.

Granzow, K. & Dean, A. (2007). Revanchism in the Canadian West: Gentrification and resettlement in a prairie city. *Topia*, 18, 89-106.

Gregory, M. (2012, May 22). City survey consults public on new arena designs. *Edmonton Journal Online*. Retrieved from: http://www.edmontonjournal.com/news/City+survey+consults+public+arena+designs/6660329/story.html.

Griffiths, C.T., & Hatch Cunningham, A. (2003) *Canadian criminal justice: A primer* (2nd ed.). Scarborough, Ontario: Nelson Canada.

Hannam, K., Sheller, M., & Urry, J. (2006). Editorial: Mobilities, immobilities and moorings. *Mobilities*, 1(1), 1-22.

Hanon, A. (2009, January 27). Aggressive panhandlers can make hundreds of dollars a day by bullying and frightening people. *Edmonton Sun Online*. Retrieved from: http://www.edmontonsun.com/news/edmonton/2009/01/27/8163076-sun.html.

Harder, L, & Trimble, L. (2005). The art of contradiction: Women in Ralph Klein's Alberta. In T. Harrison (Ed.), *The return of the Trojan horse: Albert and the new world (dis)order*, (pp. 297-312). Montreal: Black Rose Books.

Hayward, K., & Yar, M. (2006). The 'chav' phenomenon: Consumption, media and the construction of a new underclass. *Crime, Media, Culture*, 2(1), 9-28.

Hayward, K. (2004). *City limits: Crime, consumer culture and the urban experience*. London: GlassHouse Press.

Herbert, S., & Brown, E. (2006). Conceptions of space and crime in the punitive neoliberal city. *Anitpode*, 38(4), 755-777.

Hermer, J. (2001). Gift encounters: Conceptualizing the elements of begging conduct. *University of Miami Law Review*, 56(1), 77-88.

Hermer, J. (1999). Policing compassion: 'Diverted giving' on the Winchester High Street. In Hartley Dean (Ed.), *Begging Questions: Street-level Economic Activity and Social Policy Failure*, (pp. 203-218). Bristol: The Policy Press.

Hermer, J. (1997). Keeping Oshawa beautiful: Policing the loiterer in Public Nuisance By-law 72094. *Canadian Journal of Law and Society*, 12, 171-192.

Hermer, J., & Mosher, J. (2002). Introduction. In J. Hermer & J. Mosher (Eds.), *Disorderly people: Law and the politics of exclusion in Ontario*, (pp. 11-21). Halifax: Fernwood.

Ho, C. (2010, April 15). Edmonton wants task force to deal with panhandlers. *Edmonton Sun Online*. Retrieved from: http://www.edmontonsun.com/news/edmonton/2010/04/15/13600 786.html.

Ho, C. (2009, June 23). Spare the change: Proposed campaign would discourage people from giving money directly to panhandlers. *Edmonton Sun Online*. Retrieved from: http://www.edmontonsun.com/news/edmonton/2009/06/22/9884036-sun.html.

Hogeveen, B. & Freistadt, J. (2013). Hospitality to the homeless: Jacques Derrida in the neoliberal city. *Journal of Theoretical and Philosophical Criminology*, 5(1), 39-63.

Hogeveen, B., & Freistadt, J. (2012). Scarecrows and canaries: Justice and the youthful other. In R. Jochelson & K. Gorkoff (Eds.), *Thinking about justice: A book of readings* (pp. 217-237). Halifax: Fernwood.

Hogeveen, B. & Smandych, R. (2000). Origins of the newly proposed Canadian Youth Criminal Justice Act: Political discourses and the perceived crisis in youth crime in the 1990s. In R. Smandych (Ed.), *Youth justice: History, legislation, and reform*, (pp. 144-168). Toronto: Harcourt Canada.

Holstein, J., & Gubrium, J. (1995). *The active interview*. Thousand Oaks: Sage.

Homeward Trust Edmonton. (2012). *2011 annual report*. Edmonton: Homeward Trust Edmonton.

Hulchanski, J. D., Campsie, P., Chau, S., Hwang, S., & Paradis, E. (2009). Homelessness: What is in a word? In J.D. Hulchanski, P. Campsie, S. Chau, S. Hwang & E. Paradis (Eds.), *Finding Home: Policy options for addressing homelessness in Canada*, (pp. 1-16). Toronto: Cities Centre, University of Toronto.

Hwang, S. (2001). Homelessness and health. *Canadian Medical Association Journal*, 164(2), 229-233.

Hychner, R. (1985). Some guidelines for the phenomenological analysis of interview data. *Human Studies*, 8, 279-303.

Ibrahim, M. (2010, July 21). Campaign aims to reroute generosity: People asked to donate change to social agency, not panhandlers. *Edmonton Journal*, p. B3.

Jacobs, M. (2011, June 27). Feeding addiction isn't charity, it's just plain dumb. *Edmonton Sun Online*. Retrieved from: http://www.edmontonsun.com/2011/06/27/feeding-addiction-isnt-charity-its-just-plain-dumb.

James, C. (2002). "Armed and dangerous": Racializing suspects, suspecting race. In B. Schissel & C. Brooks (Eds.), *Marginality and Condemnation* (pp. 289-308). Halifax: Fernwood.

Jocoy, C., & Del Casino, V. (2010). Homelessness, travel behaviour, and the politics of transportation mobilities in Long Beach, California. *Environment and Planning A*, 42, 1943-1963.

Jordan, B. (1999). Begging: The global context and international comparisons. In H. Dean (Ed.), *Begging questions: Street-level economic activity and social policy failure*, (pp. 43-62). Bristol: The Policy Press.

Kelling, G., & Coles, C. (1997). *Fixing broken windows: Restoring order and reducing crime in our communities.* New York: The Free Press.

Kent, G. (2010, April 16). Kiosks take aim at Edmonton panhandlers: Public instead offered change to give to give to charity. *Edmonton Journal Online.* Retrieved from: http://www2.canada.com/edmontonjournal/news/story.html?id=40f514c3-6ffe-4aa8-be77-3045d15162b3.

Kent, G. (2009, October 20). City survey will get handle on panhandlers. *Edmonton Journal Online.* Retrieved from: http://www2.canada.com/edmontonjournal/news/cityplus/story.html?id=9a14ff1b-b37e-41e1-9c9b-66b36c6824f8.

Kent, G. (2008, June 20). New law won't stop panhandling, report: However, police want tougher rules. *Edmonton Journal,* p. B12.

Kent, G. (2007, June 20). Mayor says Saskatoon's approach worth exploring: Saskatchewan city's bylaw calls for fines of up to $10,000 for coercive begging. *Edmonton Journal,* p. A3.

Kent, G. (1992, December 8). Voucher system studied for inner-city panhandlers. *Edmonton Journal,* p. B2.

Kidd, S. (2012). Invited commentary seeking a coherent strategy in our response to homeless and street-involved youth: A historical review and suggested future directions. *Journal of Youth and Adolescence,* 41, 533–543.

King, W., & Dunn, T. (2004). Dumping: Police-initiated transjurisdictional transport of troublesome persons. *Police Quarterly.* 7, 339-358.

Klaszus, J. (2010, July 26). Don't vilify panhandlers. *Calgary Herald.* Retrieved from: http://www2.canada.com/calgaryherald/news/theeditorialpage/story.html?id=adfc9fd0-7a9d-45d6-abfe-f99e7b0cd2fc.

Kleiss, K. (2010, Oct. 11). Housing dollars fuel chaos: residents. *Edmonton Journal,* p. A1.

Kleiss, K. (2009, September 15). Residents tell police of 'hooligans.' *Edmonton Journal,* p. A15.

Klee, H., & Reid, P. (1998) Drug use among the young homeless: Coping through self-medication. *Health,* 2(2), 115-134.

Kline, M. (1992). Child welfare law, "best interests of the child" ideology, and First Nations. *Osgoode Hall Law Journal*, 30, 375-425.

Klodawsky, F. (2009). Home spaces and rights to the city: Thinking social justice for chronically homeless women. *Urban Geography*, 30(6), 591-610.

Kraus, D., & Graves, J. (2002). *Research project on homelessness in greater Vancouver: Vol. 3. A methodology to obtain first person qualitative information from people who are homeless and formerly homeless*. Vancouver: The Greater Vancouver Regional District.

La Prairie, C. (2002). Aboriginal over-representation in the criminal justice system: A tale of nine cities. *Canadian Journal of Criminology and Criminal Justice*, 44, 181-208.

Lafrance, Jean. (2005). Does our path have a heart? Children's Services in Alberta. In T. Harrison (Ed.), *The return of the Trojan horse: Albert and the new world (dis)order*, (pp. 269-284). Montreal: Black Rose Books.

Laird, G. (2007). *Homelessness in a growth economy: Canada's 21st century paradox*. Calgary: Sheldon Chumir Foundation for Ethics in Leadership.

Lankenau, Stephen E. (1999a). Panhandling repertoires and routines for overcoming the nonperson treatment. *Deviant Behaviour*, 20(2), 183-206.

Lankenau, S. (1999b). Stronger than dirt: Public humiliation and enhancement among panhandlers. *Journal of Contemporary Ethnography*, 28(2), 288-318.

Lawrence, B. (2002). Rewriting histories of the land: Colonization and Indigenous resistance in Eastern Canada. In Sherene Razack (Ed.), *Race, space and the law: Unmapping a White settler society*, (pp, 21-46). Toronto: Between the Lines.

Lenon, S. (2000). Living on the Edge: Women, poverty and homelessness in Canada. *Canadian Women Studies*, 20(2), 123-126.

Letkemann, P. (2004). First Nations urban migration and the importance of "urban nomads" in Canadian Plains cities: A perspective from the streets. *Canadian Journal of Urban Research*, 13(2), 241-256.

Levine-Rasky, C. (2002). Introduction. In C. Levine-Rasky (Ed.), *Working through whiteness: International perspectives*, (pp 1-24). Albany: State University of New York.

Liewicki, N. (2011, January 23). Homeless memorial casts light on forgotten deaths: Boyle Street observance remembers 57 who died on the streets last year. *Edmonton Journal*, p. A7.

Lindseth, A., & Norberg, A. (2004). A phenomenological hermeneutical method for researching lived experience. *Scandinavian Journal of Caring Science*,18, 145-153.

Lyon-Callo, V. (2000). Medicalizing homelessness: The production of self-blame and self-governing within homeless shelters. *Medical Anthropology Quarterly*, 14(3), 328-345.

May, J. (2000). Of nomads and vagrants: Single homelessness and narratives of home as place. *Environment and Planning D: Society and Space*, 18, 737-759.

MacLaurin, B. & Worthington, C. (2012). Street-involved youth in Canada. In J. Winterdyk & R. Smandych (Eds.), *Youth at risk and youth justice: A Canadian overview*, (pp. 276-306). Don Mills, Ontario: Oxford.

Martin, D. (2002). Demonizing youth, marketing fear: The new politics of crime. In J. Hermer & J. Mosher (Eds.), *Disorderly people: Law and the politics of exclusion in Ontario*, (pp. 91-104). Halifax: Fernwood.

Mawani. R. (2012). Racial violence and the cosmopolitan city. *Environment and Planning D: Society and Space*, 30, 1083-1102.

Mawani, R. (2010). 'Half-breeds,' racial opacity, and geographies of crime: Law's search for the 'original' Indian. *Cultural Geographies*, 17(4), 487-506.

Mawani, R. (2005). Genealogies of the land: Aboriginality, law, and territory in Vancouver's Stanley Park. *Social & Legal Studies*, 14(3), 315-339.

Mawani, R. (2002). "The iniquitous practice of women": Prostitution and the making of white spaces in British Columbia. In C. Levine-Rasky (Ed.), *Working through whiteness: International perspectives*, (pp 43-68). Albany: State University of New York.

Mawani, R., & Sealy, D. (2011). On postcolonialism and criminology. In K. Kramar (Ed.), *Criminology: Critical Canadian perspectives*, (pp. 159-172). Toronto: Pearson.

Mayers, M. (2001). *Street kids and streetscapes: Panhandling, politics, & prophecies*. New York: Peter Lang Publishing.

McKay Finnigan & Associates. (2010). *Final report of the Boyle Renaissance Advisory Committee II*. Edmonton: McKay Finnigan & Associates.

McKeen, S. (2008, June 27). Panhandlers need more than easy handouts: Social ill requires real effort to alleviate misery. *Edmonton Journal*, p. B1.

McKeen, S. (2006, September 13). Giving money to panhandlers doesn't help anyone. *Edmonton Journal*, p. B1.

McNeil, C. (2010). Homeless in Halifax: The criminal justice system takes aim at the poor. In D. Crocker & V.M. Johnson (Eds.), *Poverty, regulation & social justice: Readings on the criminalization of poverty*, (pp. 150-162). Halifax: Fernwood.

Meanwell, E. (2012). Experiencing homelessness: A review of recent literature. *Sociology Compass*, 6(1), 72-85.

Melrose, M. (1999). Word from the street: The perils and pains of researching begging. In Hartley Dean (Ed.), *Begging questions: Street-level economic activity and social policy failure*, (pp. 143-161). Bristol: The Policy Press.

Merleau-Ponty, M. (2002). *Phenomenology of Perception* (C. Smith, Trans.). New York: Routledge.

Miller, W., & Crabtree, B. (2004). Depth interviewing. In S. N. Hesse-Biber & P. Leavy (Eds.), *Approaches to qualitative research: A reader on theory and practice,* (pp. 185-202). New York: Oxford.

Minaker, J. & Hogeveen, B. (2009). *Youth crime and society: Issues of power and justice.* Toronto: Pearson.

Mitchell, D. (2004). *The right to the city: Social justice and the fight for public space.* New York: Guilford Press.

Mitchell, D. (1997). The annihilation of space by law: The roots and implications of anti-homeless laws in the United States. *Antipode,* 29(1), 303-335.

Mitchell, D., & Heynen, N. (2009). The geography of survival and the right to the city: Speculations on surveillance, legal innovation, and the criminalization of intervention. *Urban Geography,* 30(6), 611-632.

Montreal police wrote a record number of tickets for the homeless. (2012, February 22). *CTV News Montreal Online.* Retrieved from: http://montreal.ctvnews.ca/mobile/montreal-police-wrote-a-record-number-of-tickets-for-homeless-1.772044.

Moon, Richard. (2002). Keeping the streets safe from free expression. In J. Hermer & J. Mosher (Eds.), *Disorderly people: Law and the politics of exclusion in Ontario,* (pp. 65-78). Halifax: Fernwood.

Morin, D. (2002). Doing time. In B. Schissel & C. Brooks (Eds.), *Marginality and condemnation,* (pp. 329-347). Halifax: Fernwood.

Mosher, J. (2002). The shrinkage of the public and private spaces of the poor. In J. Hermer & J. Mosher (Eds.), *Disorderly people: Law and the politics of exclusion in Ontario,* (pp. 37-53). Halifax: Fernwood.

National Coalition for the Homeless. (2009). *Substance abuse and homelessness.* Washington: National Coalition for the Homeless.

Neocleous, M. (2006). Theoretical foundations of the "new police science." In M. Dubber & M. Valverde (Eds.), *The new police science: The police power in domestic and international governance,* (pp. 17-41). Stanford: Stanford University.

Neocleous, M. (2000). Social police and the mechanisms of prevention: Patrick Colquhoun and the condition of poverty. *British Journal of Criminology,* 40, 710-726.

Nettlebeck, A., & Smandych, R. (2010). Policing Indigenous peoples on two colonial frontiers: Australia's Mounted Police and Canada's North West Mounted Police. *Australia and New Zealand Journal of Criminology,* 43(2), 356-375.

O'Donnell, S. (2012, April 17). Melcor backs YMCS's affordable housing initiative. *Edmonton Journal Online.* Retrieved from: http://www.edmontonjournal.com/business/Melcor+backs+YMCA+affordable+housing+initiative/6475317/story.html.

O'Grady, W., & Bright, R. (2002). Squeezed to the point of exclusion: The case of Toronto squeegee cleaners. In J. Hermer & J. Mosher (Eds.), *Disorderly people: Law and the politics of exclusion in Ontario*, (pp. 23-39). Halifax: Fernwood.

O'Grady, W., Gaetz, S. & Buccieri, K. (2011). *Can I see your ID? The policing of youth homelessness in Toronto*. Toronto: Justice for Children and Youth & The Homeless Hub.

Pallas, T. (2008). *Response to City of Edmonton reports 2007PDD030 and 2007PDD031 panhandling / public disorder*. Edmonton: Edmonton Police Service. Retrieved from: http://webdocs.edmonton.ca/ OcctopusDocs/Public/COMPLETE/REPORTS/Cs/2--8-06- 23/2008PDD005Att3.doc.

Parnaby, P. (2003). Disaster through dirty windshields: Law, order and Toronto's squeegee kids. *Canadian Journal of Sociology*, 29(3), 281-307.

Perrault, S. (2009, July). The incarceration of Aboriginal people in adult correctional services. *Juristat*. Ottawa: Statistics Canada. Retrieved from: http://www.statcan.gc.ca/pub/85-002-x/2009003/article/10903- eng.htm.

Peters, E. (2012). 'I like to let them have their time'. Hidden homeless First Nations people in the city and their management of household relationships. *Social & Cultural Geography*, 13(4), 321-338.

Peters, E. & Robillard, V. (2009). "Everything you want is there": The place of the reserve in First Nations' homeless mobility, *Urban Geography*. 30(6), 652-680.

Pierce, C. (2010, June 16). Edmonton police had hotline to roust homeless: Transportation to shelters preferred option to arresting intoxicated vagrants, hearing told. *Edmonton Journal Online*. Retrieved from: http://www.edmontonjournal.com/news/Edmonton+police+hotline +roust+homeless/3157466/story.html.

Public Places Bylaw, City of Edmonton Bylaw 14614. (2009). Retrieved from: http://www.edmonton.ca/bylaws_licences/C14614.pdf.

Pratt, T., Gau, L., & Franklin, T. (2011). Key idea: The police can control crime. In T. Pratt, J. Gau, & T. Franklin (Eds.), *Key Ideas in Criminology and Criminal Justice*, (pp. 1-3-119). Los Angeles: Sage.

Province won't tear down Edmonton's tent city. (2007, July 8). *CBC News Online*. Retrieved from: http://www.cbc.ca/news/canada/ edmonton/story/2007/07/18/tent-city.html.

Rahimian, A., Wolch, J. R., & Koegel, P. (1992). A model of homeless migration: Homeless men in Skid Row, Los Angeles. *Environment and Planning A*, 2, 1317-1336.

Ranasinghe, P. (2010). Reconceptualizing vagrancy and reconstructing the vagrant: A socio-legal analysis of criminal law reform in Canada, 1953- 1972. *Osgood Hall Law Journal*, 48(1), 55-94.

Raworth, K. (2007, June 24). A legal nightmare. *Edmonton Journal*, p. A19.

Razack, S. (2002a). Gendered racial violence and spatialized justice: The murder of Pamela George. In S. Razack (Ed.), *Race, space and the law: Unmapping a White settler society*, (pp. 121-156). Toronto: Between the Lines.

Razack, S. (2002b). Introduction: When place becomes race. In S. Razack (Ed.)., *Race, space, and the law: Unmapping a White settler society*, (pp. 1-2). Toronto: Between the Lines

Retson, D. (1998, May 14). Panhandlers nailed downtown. *Edmonton Journal*, p. B7.

Rodrigues, A. (2012, June 25). Say 'no' to panhandling. *Edmonton Sun Online*. Retrieved from: http://www.edmontonsun.com/2012/06/25/say-no-to-panhandling.

Rodrigues, A. (2011, June 25). Campaign urges citizens away from panhandlers. *Edmonton Sun Online*. Retrieved from: http://m.edmontonsun.com/vip?referred=http://m.edmontonsun.co m/2011/06/25/campaign-urges-citizens-away-from-panhandlers.

Rodrigues, A. (2010, October 6). City urges Edmontonians not to pander to panhandlers. *Edmonton Examiner Online*. Retrieved from: http://www.edmontonexaminer.com/2010/10/05/city-urges-edmontonians-not-to-pander-to-panhandlers.

Rose, N. (1990). *Governing the soul: The shaping of the private self*. New York: Routledge.

Sadava, M. (2007, February 3). Police action gets support. *Edmonton Journal*, p. B1.

Safe Streets Act, SBC. (2004, c.75). Retrieved from British Columbia Queen's Printer website: http://www.bclaws.ca/EPLibraries/ bclaws_new/document/ID/freeside/00_04075_01.

Safe Streets Act, S.O. (1999, c.8). Retrieved from Service Ontario website: http://www.e-laws.gov.on.ca/html/statutes/english/elaws_statutes_ 99s08_e.htm.

Samuelson, L., & Monture-Angus, P. (2002) Aboriginal people and social control: The state, law, and "policing." In B. Schissel & C. Brooks (Eds.), *Marginality and Condemnation* (pp. 156-173). Halifax: Fernwood.

Sands, A. (2009, December 6). City shelters brace for plunge in mercury: Ready to supply extra beds for the homeless. *Edmonton Journal*, p. A1.

Sands, A. (2008, January 20). Friends light candles for 44 who lived and died on the streets. *Edmonton Journal*, p. A12.

Sands, A., & Kent, G. (2012, February 3). Katz Group hires WAM to develop land around arena. *Edmonton Journal Online*. Retrieved from: http://www.edmontonjournal.com/news/Katz+Group+hires+develo p+land+around+arena/6098082/story.html.

Schaefer, A. (2007). *The expressive liberty of beggars: Why it matters to them, and to ss.* Ottawa: Canadian Centre for Policy Alternatives.

Schafer, A. (1998). *Down and out in Winnipeg and Toronto: The ethics of legislating against panhandling.* Ottawa: Caledon Institute of Social Policy.

Service, J. (2012). *Under warrant: A review of the implementation of the Correctional Service of Canada's 'Mental Health Strategy.'* Kanata, Ontario: John Service Consulting & The Office of the Correctional Investigator.

Shantz, J. (2010). On the Streets There's No Forgetting Your Body. In D. Crocker & V.M. Johnson (Eds.). *Poverty, regulation & social Justice: Readings on the criminalization of poverty*, (pp. 178-181). Halifax: Fernwood.

Shier, M.L., Jones, M.E., & Graham, J.R. (2012). Employment difficulties experienced by employed homeless people: Labor market factors that contribute to and maintain homelessness. *Journal of Poverty*, 16(1), 27-47.

Simons, P. (2007, February 3). So maybe you're not outraged by the catch and release of street people. *Edmonton Journal*, p. B1.

Sorensen, M. (2012). *2012 Edmonton homeless count.* Edmonton: Homeward Trust Edmonton.

Sorensen, M. (2010). *2010 Edmonton homeless count.* Edmonton: Homeward Trust Edmonton.

Tanner, J. (2009). *Teenage troubles: Youth and deviance in Canada.* Oxford: Oxford.

Thomas, B. (2012). *Homelessness kills: An analysis of the mortality of homeless people in early twenty-first century England.* London: Crisis.

Thomson, J., Knutson, K., deKoning, J.N., Grekul, J., & Fawcett, D. (2010). *Housing needs of adults post-incarceration in Edmonton: Final report.* Edmonton: The Mustard Seed & The University of Alberta.

Traffic Bylaw, City of Edmonton Bylaw 5590. (2007). Retrieved from: http://www.edmonton.ca/bylaws_licences/bylaws/bylaws-t.aspx.

United States General Accounting Office. (2000). *Homelessness: Barriers to using mainstream programs.* Washington: United States General Accounting Office.

Wacquant, L. (2012). The prison is an outlaw institution. *The Howard Journal of Criminal Justice.* 51, 1-15.

Wacquant, L. (2009). *Punishing the poor: The neoliberal government of social security.* Durham: Duke University Press.

Wacquant, L. (2008). *Urban outcasts: A comparative sociology of advanced marginality.* London: Polity.

Wacquant, L. (2000). The new 'peculiar institution': On the prison as surrogate ghetto. *Theoretical Criminology*, 4(3), 377-389.

Wardhaugh, J. (1996). Homeless in Chinatown: Deviance and social control in cardboard city. *Sociology*, 30(4), 701-716.

Wardhaugh, J., & Jones, J. (1999) Begging in time and space: 'Shadow work' and the rural context. In Hartley Dean (Ed.), *Begging questions: Street-level economic activity and social policy failure*, (pp. 101-119). Bristol: The Policy Press.

Weinrath, M. (2009). Inmate perspectives on the remand crisis in Canada. *Canadian Journal of Criminology and Criminal Justice*, 51(3), 355-379.

Whiteford, M. (2010). Hot tea, dry toast and the responsibilisation of homeless people. *Social Policy and Society*, 9(2), 193-205.

Why the boom in homelessness. (2005, May 27). *Edmonton Journal*, p. A18.

Wilson, J., & Kelling, G. (1982) Broken windows: The police and neighbourhood safety. *The Atlantic*, 249, 29-38.

Wimpenny, P., & Gass, J. (2000). Interviewing in phenomenology and grounded theory: Is there a difference? Journal of Advanced Nursing, 31(6), 1485-1492.

Wittmeier, B. (2012, January 19). Finding shelter from the cold: Homeless find ways to survive bone-chilling temperatures. *Edmonton Journal Online*. Retrieved from: http://www.edmontonjournal.com/news/Finding+shelter+from+cold/6016373/story.html.

Wright, W. (2007, June 24). We don't need panhandling bylaw. *Edmonton Journal*, p. A19.

Zabjek, F. (2007, August 28). Cold nights roll in as tent city prepares to break camp Sept. 15. *Edmonton Journal*, p. B1.